SpringerBriefs in Economics

SpringerBriefs present concise summaries of cutting-edge research and practical applications across a wide spectrum of fields. Featuring compact volumes of 50 to 125 pages, the series covers a range of content from professional to academic. Typical topics might include:

- A timely report of state-of-the art analytical techniques
- A bridge between new research results, as published in journal articles, and a contextual literature review
- A snapshot of a hot or emerging topic
- An in-depth case study or clinical example
- A presentation of core concepts that students must understand in order to make independent contributions

SpringerBriefs in Economics showcase emerging theory, empirical research, and practical application in microeconomics, macroeconomics, economic policy, public finance, econometrics, regional science, and related fields, from a global author community.

Briefs are characterized by fast, global electronic dissemination, standard publishing contracts, standardized manuscript preparation and formatting guidelines, and expedited production schedules.

Biagio Bossone

Bringing Sentiment into Economic Reason

A Unified Theory of Choice, Finance, and Growth

Springer

Biagio Bossone
Rome, Italy

ISSN 2191-5504 ISSN 2191-5512 (electronic)
SpringerBriefs in Economics
ISBN 978-3-032-08616-7 ISBN 978-3-032-08617-4 (eBook)
https://doi.org/10.1007/978-3-032-08617-4

This Springer imprint is published by the registered company Springer Nature Switzerland AG
The registered company address is: Gewerbestrasse 11, 6330 Cham, Switzerland

To my wife Ornella and my son Blasco, the Loves of my Life

Preface

This book was not planned. Nor would I have embarked on a new demanding project immediately after completing my intensive work on money.[1] It emerged—almost instinctively—at a time when personal reflection met a long-standing intellectual intuition. I had just completed an article on the role of sentiment in macroeconomic behavior. Professor Roger Farmer, reviewing it, encouraged me to expand the ideas into a full-length book. Within a few intense weeks, I found myself laying the foundations for a general approach to macroeconomic theory that I had long felt was missing.

The result is this book, which introduces **SAGE**—the **S**entiment-**A**ugmented **G**eneral **E**quilibrium framework. More than a new model, SAGE is a proposal for unification. It brings together three foundational yet traditionally fragmented domains of macroeconomics: intertemporal choice, finance, and growth theory. Developed in isolation, these strands have struggled to explain persistent real-world phenomena: excess asset price volatility, sentiment-driven booms and busts, secular stagnation, financial crises, unstable growth, declining labor participation, and inflation, driven by shifts in asset demand.

SAGE addresses this fragmentation by building a utility-based structure in which all assets—money, bonds, capital—are valued for their liquidity, volatility, and usefulness. Expectations are shaped not only by information and knowledge, but also by confidence, mood, and collective narratives. Sentiment and reason interact dynamically to form expectations about the future—and these sentiment-contingent expectations, in turn, shape present economic behavior.

The idea is simple yet ambitious: economic agents are not disembodied calculators navigating a deterministic reality. Their decisions under uncertainty are guided by logic and emotion, trust and doubt, memory and imagination. SAGE formalizes this by integrating sentiment into both the utility calculus and expectations formation, allowing the model to account for rational yet sentiment-contingent equilibria,

[1] See Bossone (2025).

endogenous financial frictions, and nonlinear transitions such as stagnation traps and bubbles. It does so through a common metric—utility—that lets agents evaluate the value they derive from producing, exchanging, and consuming across time, states of nature, and under deep uncertainty.

In this way, SAGE bridges micro-level decision-making and macro-financial outcomes, and reconnects economics with the psychological and the social.

This book is not merely a technical exercise; it is also a personal endeavor, which I dedicate to Ornella and Blasco—my wife and son—whose love motivates my work. I chose to begin with a poem inspired by them. What better way to open a book on the fusion of reason and sentiment than through poetry?

If SAGE aspires to unify the analytical structure of economic theory, it does so in the belief that economics must also reconnect with its human roots. In a world shaped by volatility, mistrust, and fast-moving narratives, economic science must learn to listen again—to voices, to moods, and to uncertainty as it is truly experienced.

This book does not claim to offer all the answers. But it seeks to reframe the questions in a way that reflects the complexity, cognition, institutions, and emotions that define our economic lives. If it serves as a step toward a more integrated, realistic, and humane economics—one that embraces the unity of structure and sentiment—then it will have fulfilled its purpose.

Rome, Italy
August 2025

Biagio Bossone

References

Bossone, B. (2025). Trailblazing Visions of Money in Economic Theory: Essence, Genesis, and Economic Ramifications. Contributions to Economics. Springer International Publishing, Cham.

GB ***I WISH***

Written while traveling between Rome, Doha, Port Moresby, and Hong Kong—September 2024

(thinking of my wife and my son…and of Albert Camus…)

I wish I could forever hold
a moment from our everyday life.
I wish we could clasp each other
in an endless embrace.
I wish to have a bond
that time could never break.
I wish our inner selves
would never stop feeling each other.
But it's like wishing a happy dream
won't vanish at dawn,
or a radiant day
won't fade to dusk.
These are wishes for a god who isn't there.
In his place,
in my soul,
only the burden of life that perishes—
of which Reason tells me
nothing but the Absurd.

IT ***VORREI***

Composta in viaggio tra Roma, Doha, Port Moresby e Hong Kong—settembre 2024 (pensando a mia moglie e a mio figlio…e ad Albert Camus…)

Vorrei fissare per sempre
un istante della nostra vita di ogni giorno.
Vorrei ci stringessimo
in un abbraccio infinito.
Vorrei sentire un legame
che il tempo non interrompesse.
Vorrei che le nostre coscienze
mai smettessero di percepirsi.
Ma è come chiedere che un sogno felice
non si dissolva al risveglio,
o che un giorno luminoso
non volga poi al suo tramonto.
Son desideri per un dio che non c'è.
Al suo posto,
nella mia anima,
solo il gravare della vita che perisce,
di cui Ragione mi dice non altro che
l'Assurdo.

Acknowledgments

I would like to express my sincere appreciation to Roger Farmer for his suggestions and, more importantly, for suggesting me to embark on the journey of writing this book and for recommending its publication. Without his encouragement, it might never have come to fruition. I am also grateful to the various anonymous referees who provided insights on my earlier works that had formed the foundation for this book. I take full responsibility for the opinions expressed here and for any remaining errors, and I want to clarify that the views represented do not necessarily reflect those of any institutions with which I am affiliated. I also want to convey a special thanks to my dear friend and worldly renowned writer, Jhumpa Lahiri, for her help in translating the small poem at the beginning of this book from Italian to English. Her skillful interpretation beautifully captures the essence of the original text. Lastly, I am profoundly thankful to my wife, Ornella, for her unwavering support and love, which have been my constant source of strength throughout my research journey. Her belief in me has always been an anchor as I navigated this endeavor and all the preceding ones. This book would not have been possible without the support of Johannes Glaeser and his colleagues at Springer Nature, who accompanied the project from concept to realisation. I am deeply grateful to all of them.

About the Book

This book introduces **SAGE**—the **S**entiment-**A**ugmented **G**eneral **E**quilibrium framework—as a unified theory of inter-temporal choice, finance, and economic growth. At its core lies the dynamic interplay between reason and sentiment: agents form expectations not only through structural knowledge and observable data, but also via psychological states, market moods, and socially mediated narratives. These expectations, in turn, shape agents' current sentiment, generating feedback loops that drive economic behavior. SAGE embeds financial frictions—such as asset liquidation costs, price volatility, and the quality of intermediation—directly into the utility calculus, linking sentiment and expectations dynamics to consumption, portfolio allocation, and labor supply decisions. This allows the model to endogenize how changes in sentiment-contingent expectations affect the agents' intra- and inter-temporal utility and, through their choices, aggregate macroeconomic outcomes. The framework naturally extends to overlapping generations, enabling a structural analysis of demographic trends, belief persistence, and age-dependent macro-financial patterns. Employing a parsimonious yet expressive modeling strategy, SAGE offers a psychologically and socially grounded explanation—recognizing sentiment as both an individual disposition and a collectively constructed force—for key macroeconomic phenomena, including boom–bust cycles, prolonged stagnation, asset mispricing, inflation dynamics, and long-run growth. The result is a flexible, tractable, and extensible framework that opens new frontiers for theoretical modeling, empirical inquiry, and policy design in a sentiment-driven economy.

Contents

Chapter 1
Introduction

«The heart has its reasons of which reason knows nothing...»
Pascal, Pensées, trans. A. J. Krailsheimer, Penguin Classics, 1966, fragment 423.

Contents

Abstract The introduction sets the stage for the Sentiment-Augmented General Equilibrium (SAGE) framework by identifying a core shortcoming in economic theory: its failure to integrate the roles of human sentiment and intertemporal choice into a unified, microfounded structure. It addresses the segmentation between choice and price theory, finance, and growth theory, and argues that conventional frameworks—such as dynamic stochastic general equilibrium and asset-pricing models—struggle to account for real-world anomalies like prolonged stagnation, asset mispricing, unstable growth, and labor force withdrawal. SAGE addresses this gap by developing a utility-based model in which all assets—including money, bonds, and capital—deliver utility conditional on liquidation costs and price volatility. The chapter introduces the central innovation of treating sentiment not as irrational noise but as a state variable that co-evolves with rational expectations. It outlines how sentiment and reason jointly determine agents' belief structures and portfolio allocations, which in turn shape macroeconomic equilibria. The

B. Bossone, *Bringing Sentiment into Economic Reason*, SpringerBriefs in Economics, https://doi.org/10.1007/978-3-032-08617-4_1

introduction presents SAGE as both a conceptual framework and an operational tool, capable of explaining macro-financial phenomena as endogenous responses to sentiment-influenced expectations. Finally, it positions SAGE within a broader scientific ambition: to unify disparate strands of economic thought under a psychologically grounded and empirically relevant theory of decision-making, finance, and growth.

At its heart, this book addresses a foundational challenge in economics: the lack of a coherent theoretical framework capable of explaining how individual decisions under uncertainty—driven by both reason and sentiment—aggregate into the complex macroeconomic dynamics observed in the real world. The book introduces the **S**entiment-**A**ugmented **G**eneral **E**quilibrium (SAGE) framework to re-integrate macroeconomics from the ground up. SAGE builds on a recognition that utility lies at the core of economic behavior, and that all goods, services, financial instruments, and productive assets, or otherwise, available in an economy can all be meaningfully compared to each other, intra-temporally and inter-temporally, based on their respective contribution to the utility that each of them delivers to their holders By treating sentiment, liquidity, financial structure, and macroeconomic growth as endogenous and interdependent, SAGE provides a flexible yet rigorous architecture for analyzing a wide range of economic facts and phenomena through a single, integrated lens.

The scientific effort to unify fragmented strands of economic theory through SAGE rests on three foundational concepts: reason, sentiment, and utility. The first two—reason and sentiment—interact dynamically and together constitute the cognitive-affective essence of human agency. The third, utility, serves as the encompassing, universal metric through which all economic objects and activities are evaluated and chosen by agents acting under uncertainty.

1.1 Fragmented Foundations of Modern Economics

Modern macroeconomics remains deeply segmented across its foundational domains—intertemporal choice theory (borrowed from microeconomics), financial economics, and growth theory. Each field traditionally employs distinct assumptions and tools, resulting in macroeconomic models that lack a truly unified perspective on how people acting under uncertainty allocate their wealth intra- and inter-temporally, between consumption and different asset classes, and how their allocation decisions drive long-term growth. Neither standard dynamic stochastic general equilibrium (DSGE) models nor other frameworks fully integrate asset-market behavior or persistent liquidity traps: these paradigms generally presume that, given enough time (and perhaps some policy adjustments), economies return to full-employment equilibrium, which leaves them ill-equipped to explain prolonged stagnations of the kind seen in Japan or post-2008 Europe. Likewise, canonical asset-pricing models (e.g., the consumption capital asset-pricing model, CCAPM, see Sects. 2.1–2.2) require ad hoc fixes—such as extreme risk aversion, habit formation, or "rare disaster" shocks—to match empirical puzzles.

This fragmentation began to be addressed with the rise of New Classical Economics in the 1970s and 1980s, which, as Arie Arnon (2022) emphasizes, marked a pivotal moment in the unification of economic theory. New Classical economics integrated microeconomic foundations into macroeconomics by embedding intertemporal choice and price theory and rational expectations at the heart of dynamic models, and it contributed significantly to the theoretical consolidation of choice and growth. Yet while this unification—which was then inherited by the New Keynesian articulation of New Classical economics—brought analytical coherence to mainstream macroeconomic models, it left financial choices largely underdeveloped and treated assets narrowly as budgetary tools rather than utility-bearing options. SAGE moves decisively beyond this legacy in two ways: first, by systematically incorporating financial choices into the model of the economy, and second, by using utility as the common intra- and inter-temporal metric to compare all allocable resources—consumption goods and services, money, and the full spectrum of assets—based on their relative liquidity and value-storing capacity. In doing so, SAGE extends the microfoundational revolution to encompass the full set of household portfolio decisions, enabling a richer and more realistic theory of macroeconomic dynamics. Also, by incorporating sentiment and its dynamic interaction with reason into a general equilibrium framework, SAGE enables the existence of multiple equilibria, including with resource underemployment. This capability is entirely lacking in New Classical economics, while New Keynesian economics can only replicate it by introducing exogenous, ad hoc frictions into its models.

1.2 The Need for Further Integration: Enter SAGE

This intellectual fragmentation has created a need for a unifying framework that can bridge microeconomic choices, asset-market dynamics, and macroeconomic outcomes within a single coherent structure. The SAGE framework proposed in this book aims to fill this gap. SAGE fuses together the theories of intertemporal choice, portfolio allocations, and endogenous growth. At its core is a utility-theoretic foundation broad enough to make all traded items—from consumption goods and services to money, bonds, and productive capital—mutually comparable in terms of the utility they deliver intra-temporally and inter-temporally to their holders. In other words, everything that agents hold or trade is modeled as yielding utility, either directly or through future consumption opportunities. By treating different assets as competing "vehicles" that enable their holders to carry forward access to real resources across time and states of nature, each with its own "speed" and "power," SAGE creates a common language for analyzing decisions that were previously compartmentalized (see Sect. 3.1).

1.3 Human Sentiment and Rational Expectations

In human behavior, reason and sentiment are not simply coexisting faculties—they are deeply interwoven in a relation of reciprocal dependency, where each draws strength and meaning from the other. Reason is not autonomous or self-sufficient: it feeds on sentiment—sensations, emotions, and passions—that provide the living matter through which thought is oriented and value is assigned. At the same time, sentiment is never pure instinct; it involves a layer of reflection, of reasoning, that makes it intelligible and communicable. This mutual interpenetration is not neutral. Sentiment can guide reason toward creative, constructive aims, as when enlightened passion inspires generous and visionary action. Or it can distort judgment, as unregulated emotion steers rationality toward error or harm. Likewise, reason can elevate and refine sentiment, or, conversely, suppress and deform it. It is in this dynamic (dis)equilibrium—made of tension and harmony—that the true nature of human decision-making emerges, grounded in the never-final synthesis of heart and mind.

A distinguishing feature of SAGE is its treatment of human sentiment alongside rationality in economic decision-making. Drawing on evidence from neuroscience and behavioral science that emotion and reason are inextricably linked (Forgas, 2001), SAGE explicitly builds sentiment into agents' expectations and vice versa. Formally, expectations are rational (agents use all available information and the model's structure), but they are also exposed to sentiment—meaning, for instance, that optimism or pessimism about the future affects how agents use their knowledge and information to forecast and plan. Similarly, agents' expectations of the future based on current knowledge and information shape their current sentiment. This approach contrasts with both classical models (which assume coolly rational expectations unaffected by emotions) and purely behavioral models (which might allow sentiment-influenced biases but often abandon rational expectations altogether).

SAGE does not merely allow sentiment to play a role; it treats sentiment as a formal state variable. This modeling strategy enables the framework to endogenously generate phenomena like boom–bust cycles, self-reinforcing pessimism, and multiple equilibria driven by shifts in expectations. Sentiment responds not only to fundamentals, but to the unfolding macro-financial environment itself, making it both a driver and a consequence of economic dynamics, and shape agent expectations built on the information and knowledge available. The economy's trajectory becomes contingent on how sentiment and reason interact: given the same structural fundamentals, different interactions—driven by different individual and/or social factors—can result in dramatically different equilibrium outcomes.

1.4 Methodological Innovations

Methodologically, SAGE introduces several innovations beyond standard macro-financial models. First, it generalizes the utility function to include assets as arguments, alongside consumption and leisure. This endogenously explains asset demand shifts under different economic conditions, providing a rigorous foundation for asset-based utility that extends the classic money-in-the-utility and cash-in-advance approaches.

Second, expectations are modeled as a dynamic feedback system shaped by endogenous sentiment—endogenous in the sense that it responds to new information. Rather than being passively calibrated to external shocks, expectations in SAGE amplify or dampen disturbances depending on sentiment dynamics. Rational expectations allow the model to capture asset bubbles, liquidity traps, and self-fulfilling cycles without abandoning microfoundations.

Third, SAGE offers an endogenous treatment of financial frictions. Asset liquidation costs and price volatility are not exogenously imposed but arise, inter alia, from institutional and market structure—including depth, trust, and quality of financial intermediation (see Sect. 3.1). Thus, SAGE internalizes financial infrastructure into the utility calculus, showing how institutional weakness (strength) translates into macroeconomic fragility (stability).

These innovations collectively distinguish SAGE from New Keynesian DSGE models, which typically treat financial frictions as static parameters or exogenous wedges, as well as from canonical asset-pricing models that rely on restrictive utility functions and implausible assumptions to explain return patterns. SAGE provides a richer, more realistic framework in which economic agents, facing an uncertain future, derive utility from everything they produce, exchange, and consume within the economy, as well as from money and other assets they hold. In this framework, institutions, frictions, sentiments, and expectations interact endogenously to shape macroeconomic trajectories.

1.5 Testable Predictions

While SAGE is fundamentally a theoretical construct, it generates a wide range of empirically testable predictions. These include the sensitivity of asset demand to liquidity and price volatility, the co-movement of sentiment indices and portfolio allocations, and the amplification of shocks through endogenous sentiment dynamics. Moreover, it predicts cross-country variation in macroeconomic performances based on institutional quality, financial infrastructure, and policy credibility. These implications open up new avenues for empirical research and policy evaluation using sentiment indicators, asset-market data, and structural estimation techniques (see Chap. 6). SAGE also yields testable predictions regarding labor force participation, particularly among prime-age workers, as driven by sentiment-contingent job valuation.

1.6 A Complex Systems Perspective

SAGE brings macroeconomic theory closer to the realities of complex adaptive systems. By acknowledging endogenous expectations, multiple equilibria, and recursive feedbacks, the framework departs from the simplifying assumptions of representative-agent models and certainty-equivalence analysis. It models economies as dynamic systems in which agents continuously update their sentiments, portfolios, and expectations in response to both objective conditions and evolving narratives. This complexity-aware foundation offers a new epistemological stance for macroeconomics—one that aligns more closely with observed behavior in financial markets, historical crises, and real-world institutions.

It is important to stress, however, that while SAGE acknowledges the explanatory power of complexity-based approaches—such as recursive dynamics, endogenous feedbacks, and multiple equilibria—it does not build upon complexity theory in the sense defined by Colander (2009). Instead, it pursues analytical parsimony, integrating sentiment and institutional structure directly into a tractable utility-based framework. The aim is to explain the most with the least: to reproduce key anomalies in macro-financial behavior without resorting to high-dimensional simulations or network-based interactions. This choice is deliberate, enabling a clearer focus on the conceptual unification of choice, finance, and growth within an equilibrium framework.

In addition, while the SAGE framework in its current form relies on a representative-agent formulation, with the known limitations of that abstraction, it nonetheless provides a valid structure for analyzing economies in which sentiment-contingent rational expectations are broadly shared across agents—either because of common information sets, institutional coordination, or demographic uniformity. As discussed in Chap. 6, extending the model to accommodate heterogeneous agents is both desirable and necessary for a fuller understanding of distributional dynamics and belief diversity. However, even within a representative-agent setup, the model is methodologically adequate for capturing scenarios in which distinct agent groups—despite their heterogeneity—temporarily align in their expectations and preferences due to prevailing macro-sentiment regimes. Such alignment may occur in the short run, when agents react similarly to market signals, news, or policy shifts; or in the long run, when demographic structures (e.g., aging populations) shape aggregate sentiment toward prudence, risk aversion, and shortened time horizons. In these settings, the representative agent serves as a stylized but meaningful proxy for collective behavior, allowing the model to capture the macroeconomic implications of coordinated shifts in sentiment and expectations.

1.7 Resolving Puzzles and Synthesizing Paradigms

SAGE provides unified solutions to long-standing puzzles, as shall be seen in Sect. 3.2. The equity premium puzzle is resolved through endogenous disutility of volatile, illiquid capital; exchange rate overshooting arises as a rational portfolio shift under sentiment shock; and secular stagnation becomes a sentiment-contingent equilibrium. SAGE synthesizes Keynesian concerns about liquidity preference with neoclassical intertemporal optimization and financial theory's attention to asset demand and pricing.

SAGE's structure allows it to explain why economies may settle in inefficient yet stable equilibria, such as stagnation traps, even when fundamentals are sound, and why international capital flows may be subject to sudden changes or may follow counterintuitive directions as a result of changes in prevailing investor sentiment. Unlike models that require implausibly persistent shocks or rule out nonlinear dynamics, SAGE accommodates hysteresis, regime shifts, and endogenous volatility as natural outcomes of optimizing behavior in a world with an uncertain and unknowable future, where sentiment interacts continuously with rational expectations.

SAGE also explains recent structural labor market phenomena—such as post-crisis declines in participation—not as mechanical outcomes of demographic trends or productivity, but as sentiment-contingent equilibria where sentiment shapes the perceived utility of work.

In addition, SAGE offers a novel account of inflation persistence and regime shifts due to portfolio reallocations. It explains how inflation may remain stubbornly low when pessimism leads agents to hoard liquidity despite low interest rates, and conversely how inflation can surge when optimism detaches expectations from fundamentals. These are not mere anomalies but sentiment-contingent equilibria under uncertainty.

Finally, the SAGE framework can be extended to an overlapping generations structure, allowing for demographic heterogeneity, intergenerational sentiment propagation, and life-cycle portfolio behavior. This formulation makes it possible to endogenize expectations hysteresis, demographic stagnation traps, and cohort-specific policy responses within the SAGE architecture.

1.8 Real-World Motivations

The realism and relevance of SAGE are grounded in historical experience showing dynamics generated by self-reinforcing pessimism, hoarding of liquid assets, collapse of investment, and protracted stagnation. Standard models assume convergence, whereas SAGE explains persistent divergence as equilibrium.

For example, Japan's post-bubble stagnation is easily interpreted as a sentiment-contingent equilibrium under SAGE, where pessimism about future returns on capital induced a prolonged preference for liquidity. Similarly, the slow Eurozone recovery after 2008, despite low interest rates, reflects portfolio choices in the face of credibility and institutional fragmentation. Even the Great Depression, with its massive collapse in investment and spike in money hoarding, aligns with SAGE mechanisms: confidence shocks altered the utility of different asset classes and restructured portfolio allocations in a way that became self-reinforcing.

The real-world relevance of SAGE is further reinforced by its capacity to reinterpret labor force withdrawal, financial fragility, and inflation as phenomena influenced by sentiment.

1.9 Scope and Limitations

SAGE, by design, carries substantial implications for economic policymaking. Its structure offers a fresh lens through which to interpret the transmission and credibility of fiscal, monetary, and macroprudential policies. In the SAGE world, policy effectiveness hinges not only on conventional levers but also on how these levers interact with expectations, liquidity preferences, and institutional structures. Central bank communication, the robustness of financial intermediation, and long-run credibility are no longer auxiliary concerns—they become central elements that shape agents' portfolios, investment horizons, and ultimately macroeconomic performance.

Yet, while these policy insights follow naturally from SAGE's structure, this book does not attempt to offer a policy blueprint. Instead, its purpose is to establish and articulate the theoretical foundations of the framework. The goal is to construct a flexible and internally consistent model that can serve as a basis for subsequent applications—whether empirical, computational, or policy-oriented. Accordingly, concrete policy discussions, such as the calibration of sentiment-responsive interest rate rules, liquidity regulation, or fiscal multipliers under sentiment volatility, are left to future work. This strategic deferral reflects a recognition that robust policy analysis must rest on a well-understood theoretical architecture—precisely what this book aims to deliver.

1.10 A Broader Scientific Ambition

SAGE aspires to do for macroeconomics what unifying theories have accomplished in the natural sciences. Since antiquity, humans have longed to uncover the hidden unity behind nature and society. From Newton's laws to the search for a Grand Unified Theory in physics, unification has long been a marker of scientific maturity. What distinguishes a science as it evolves is not only its growing empirical accuracy but also its capacity to reveal deep structural connections across seemingly disparate phenomena. In this regard, unification signals the moment when a discipline begins to see itself not merely as a collection of models or empirical regularities, but as a coherent worldview grounded in a shared theoretical foundation (Box 1.1).

Box 1.1 The Long Pursuit of Scientific Unification
From the apple that fell on Newton's head to the equations that describe the movement of stars, the ambition to reduce the cosmos to coherent principles has propelled science forward. This enduring dream has shaped centuries of inquiry across disciplines—Sometimes in triumph, sometimes in tension.

Physics has often led the charge. Newton's unification of gravity and motion (Newton, 1687), Maxwell's marriage of light and electromagnetism (Maxwell, 1865), and Einstein's fusion of space and time (Einstein, 1905, 1915) revealed profound symmetries. The twentieth century saw further breakthroughs: the electroweak theory unified two of the fundamental forces (Glashow, 1961; Weinberg, 1967), and Grand Unified Theories sought to include the strong nuclear force. Yet the final step—reconciling gravity with quantum mechanics—remains a daunting frontier. String theory and quantum gravity offer tantalizing glimpses, but the ultimate Theory of Everything still hovers at the edge of scientific imagination.

Biology has followed a more intricate and layered path. Darwin's theory of natural selection (Darwin, 1859) provided a sweeping explanatory arc for the diversity of life. Later, the modern synthesis with Mendelian genetics brought molecular clarity. In recent decades, new forms of synthesis have emerged—from systems biology and the study of self-organization to thermodynamic approaches to life. Schrödinger's insight that organisms feed on "negative entropy" (Schrödinger, 1944) and Jeremy England's hypothesis that life may arise from energy dissipation (England, 2013) suggest a growing overlap between biology and the physics of information.

The social sciences, however, have proven more resistant to unification. Auguste Comte dreamed of a positivist hierarchy culminating in sociology (Comte, 1830–1842). Karl Marx envisioned history as the unfolding of material dialectics (Marx, 1859). In the twentieth century, Paul Samuelson gave economics a formal structure modeled on classical mechanics (Samuelson, 1947), but critics like Mark Granovetter emphasized the social embeddedness of economic action (Granovetter, 1985). Human behavior, embedded in culture, language, and institutions, resists reduction to a universal calculus.

Still, unifying tendencies persist. Computational social science has emerged as a bridge across economics, sociology, and political science, grounded in data and modeling (Lazer et al., 2009). Unified Growth Theory traces the long arc of human history through demography, innovation, and inequality (Galor, 2011). And interdisciplinary frameworks like quantum social science (Haven & Khrennikov, 2013), econophysics (Mantegna &

(continued)

Box 1.1 (continued)
Stanley, 2000), and complexity theory increasingly blur the line between physical and social domains.

Unification, then, remains a story in motion. It is not about forcing all science into one mold, but about crafting structures that reveal deep coherence amid complexity. The pursuit invites humility—An acknowledgment that final synthesis may never be fully achieved—And ambition, a commitment to expand our understanding through connection, analogy, and dialogue across domains.

SAGE proposes a unifying framework for economics, whereby consumption, portfolio choices, sentiment dynamics, and economic growth interact through a common theoretical language. By grounding its unification in utility and sentiment-contingent rational expectations, SAGE seeks to lay the groundwork for a more integrated economic science. Crucially, this unification does not rely on the assumption that agents are purely rational calculators. Drawing on a growing body of evidence from behavioral economics, psychology, and neuroscience, SAGE recognizes that human reason and sentiment are not separable domains but are deeply intertwined. Sentiments are shaped not only by information and inference but also by confidence, narratives, and emotion—factors that influence how agents interpret uncertainty and make forward-looking decisions. By embedding this emotional-cognitive interplay directly into the structure of utility and expectations formation, SAGE captures the real-world dynamics of macro-financial behavior more fully than models that treat sentiment as exogenous or irrational. In doing so, it advances a vision of macroeconomics that is not only unified but also psychologically and socially grounded.

The ambition of this work is evident, and I do not take lightly the historical weight of invoking scientific unification. I am acutely aware that the great breakthroughs in physics or biology were the product of generations of cumulative insight and extraordinary minds. My aim is not to claim a comparable legacy, but to take a modest step toward greater coherence in economic thought—recognizing that real progress often begins by reframing persistent questions rather than resolving them outright.

SAGE is offered as a foundational step toward an integrated economic science—one that recognizes the interdependence of utility, sentiment, and institutional structure in shaping macroeconomic outcomes. While open to refinement, it lays down a tractable, microfounded architecture capable of explaining real-world economic phenomena, and apparent anomalies, through endogenous, sentiment-contingent mechanisms. In this sense, SAGE is not merely a model, but a new lens through which to reframe enduring questions in macroeconomics.

1.11 Notes on Terminology

Throughout the book, the term *"sentiment"* is used for the sake of brevity and stylistic economy. However, as shall become clearer from Sect. 3.1 onward, readers should interpret it in a broader and more nuanced sense. *Sentiment*, as used in the book, should be read as shorthand for the ongoing dynamic interplay between affective orientation and rational information processing and action deliberation.

Importantly, this book distinguishes the word "*sentiment*" from the more narrowly defined notions of "*emotion*" and "*mood*." In psychological terms, *emotions* are short-lived, intense responses to specific stimuli, while *moods* are more diffuse and longer-lasting affective states, often without a clear cause. The concept of *sentiment* used in SAGE builds upon both but goes beyond them: it emerges from their interaction with cognition, narrative framing, and social dynamics. It is precisely this entangled structure—spanning sentiment and reason—that gives rise to sentiment-contingent rational expectations in SAGE.

The same interpretive care applies to this book's use of the expressions *"sentiment-contingent,"* "*sentiment-driven,"* and "*sentiment-adjusted*." While the three expressions appear in the text, their usage is deliberate and context-dependent. As a rule, preference is given to the expression *"sentiment-contingent"* to emphasize that rational expectations are formed within, and conditioned by, prevailing sentiment regimes—without implying that sentiment necessarily overrides reason. The expression "*sentiment-driven"* is instead used when the context justifies highlighting the leading influence of sentiment in particular circumstances, such as collective exuberance, panic, or sharp shifts in expectations formation. Furthermore, the expression "*sentiment-adjustment*" is referred more specifically to mathematical functions whose arguments are influenced by sentiment. In some cases, the expressions "*sentiment-induced,*" "*sentiment-influenced,*" or *"sentiment-responsive"* are used to convey a softer, yet still effective, role of sentiment in shaping expectations, decisions, or equilibria. In all cases, the book maintains the foundational assumption that sentiment and reason are co-constitutive rather than hierarchically ordered, and that their mutual entanglement defines the architecture of expectations, decisions, and systemic dynamics in SAGE.

1.12 Organization of the Book

The structure of this book is designed to guide the reader through the progressive development of SAGE. After this introduction, Chap. 2 provides a critical review of the relevant literature, spanning intertemporal utility theory, heterogeneous-agent macroeconomics, portfolio theory, asset pricing, and endogenous growth. It also draws on insights from behavioral economics, cognitive neuroscience, neurobiology, and statistical physics to highlight the conceptual fragmentation that SAGE seeks to overcome. Chapter 3 lays out the general structure of SAGE. It introduces the money and asset utility framework and describes the fundamental components of the economy, including the representative household and firm, production technologies, government, central bank, and financial markets. It articulates the portfolio-based view of choices and provides a unified specification of the agent's intra- and inter-temporal utility function over consumption, money, bonds, capital, and labor. The chapter also defines the asset space, the price system, and the key frictions—such as liquidation costs and volatility—that shape portfolio decisions and the dynamics of the real economy. Chapter 4 applies SAGE to key economic facts and phenomena, ranging from booms and busts, to secular stagnation, asset price and exchange rate dynamics, the impact of financial frictions, financial capital flows, growth, labor issues, and inflation. Chapter 5 conducts a thought experiment to examine whether the SAGE framework could have anticipated the 2007–09 global financial crisis. Chapter 6 points to future research trajectories that highlight SAGE's adaptive power. Chapter 7 concludes the book, synthesizing its core contributions. The appendices develop the conceptual and analytical foundations of SAGE, covering (i) the role of sentiment and reason in utility, (ii) the construction of the sentiment variable, (iii) the derivation of the reduced-form asset utility function, (iv) asset preference weights, (v) the valuation of employment, (vi) the existence of critical sentiment thresholds driving regime shifts, and (vii) the stability conditions for the capital-sentiment dynamics.

References

Arnon, A. (2022). *Debates in macroeconomics from the great depression to the long recession: Cycles, crises and policy responses* (Springer studies in the history of economic thought). Springer Nature.

Colander, D. C. (2009). Complexity and the history of economic thought, Chap. 16. In J. B. Rosser Jr. (Ed.), *Handbook of research on complexity* (pp. 409–426). Edward Elgar.

Comte, A. (1830–1842). *Cours de philosophie positive*. Bachelier.

Darwin, C. (1859). *On the origin of species by means of natural selection*. John Murray.

Einstein, A. (1905). Zur Elektrodynamik bewegter Körper. *Annalen der Physik, 17*(10), 891–921.

Einstein, A. (1915). Die Feldgleichungen der Gravitation. *Sitzungsberichte der Preussischen Akademie der Wissenschaften*, 844–847.

England, J. L. (2013). Statistical physics of self-replication. *The Journal of Chemical Physics, 139*(12), 121923.

Forgas, J. P. (2001). Introduction: Affect and Social Cognition. *Handbook of Affect and Social Cognition Mahwah, NJ: Lawrence Erlbaum Associates*, 1–24.

Galor, O. (2011). *Unified growth theory*. Princeton University Press.

Glashow, S. L. (1961). Partial-symmetries of weak interactions. *Nuclear Physics, B22*, 579–588.

Granovetter, M. (1985). Economic action and social structure: The problem of embeddedness. *American Journal of Sociology, 91*(3), 481–510.

Haven, E., & Khrennikov, A. (2013). *Quantum social science*. Cambridge University Press.

Lazer, D., Pentland, A., Adamic, L., Aral, S., Barabási, A. L., Brewer, D., Christakis, N., Contractor, N., Fowler, J., Gutmann, M., Jebara, T., King, G., Macy, M., Roy, D., & Van Alstyne, M. (2009). Computational social science. *Science, 323*(5915), 721–723.

Mantegna, R. N., & Stanley, H. E. (2000). *An introduction to econophysics: Correlations and complexity in finance*. Cambridge University Press.

Marx, K. (1859). *A contribution to the critique of political economy*. Franz Duncker.
Maxwell, J. C. (1865). A dynamical theory of the electromagnetic field. *Philosophical Transactions of the Royal Society of London, 155*, 459–512.
Newton, I. (1687). *Philosophiæ Naturalis Principia Mathematica*. Royal Society.
Samuelson, P. A. (1947). *Foundations of economic analysis*. Harvard University Press.
Schrödinger, E. (1944). *What is life? The physical aspect of the living cell*. Cambridge University Press.
Weinberg, S. (1967). A model of leptons. *Physical Review Letters, 19*, 1264–1266.

Chapter 2
Review of the Literature

Contents

Abstract This chapter reviews separately the literatures on choice and price theory, with its emphasis on utility and profit maximization; asset pricing, focused on returns and risk; and growth theory, which largely ignores individual choices and prices, financial structure and expectations. The chapter evaluates previous partial attempts at integration but shows how these either ignore sentiment or lack unifying microfoundations. The final section draws on behavioral economics, neuroeconomics, and affective science to underscore how sentiment and cognition co-determine expectations under uncertainty. It highlights how emotional orientation shapes rational expectations formation, risk perceptions, and utility evaluation. Collectively, these reviews underscore the need for a unified theory that endogenizes sentiment, links portfolio allocation to utility, and integrates growth and macro-financial dynamics. This is the space SAGE aims to occupy, offering a coherent and tractable framework that builds upon—but moves beyond—these fragmented strands.

The development of SAGE draws on four long-standing and largely disjoint literatures: (1) the theory of money as an argument in the utility function; (2) the evolution and methodological divergence of choice and price theory, financial economics, and growth theory; (3) partial or sector-specific attempts at integration; and (4) the entwinement of reason and sentiment in economic decision-making. This chapter reviews each strand and clarifies both the intellectual gaps that motivate SAGE and the ways in which it builds upon—and transcends—existing paradigms.

B. Bossone, *Bringing Sentiment into Economic Reason*, SpringerBriefs in Economics, https://doi.org/10.1007/978-3-032-08617-4_2

2.1 Money in the Utility Function

To understand the value of money in terms of the subjective utility of holding it, one must refer to the Austrian school, which traces the origin of money to the emergence of the most marketable good in barter exchange (Menger, 1892; Mises, 1912). According to this view, money arises as the most marketable good within barter economies, and its value is rooted not in intrinsic utility but in the indirect utility deriving from its capacity to facilitate exchange. This perspective was later expanded by Mises (1912) through the regression theorem, which anchors the purchasing power of money in historical marginal utility—the knowledge of its purchasing power in the past, i.e., money has value today because it had value yesterday. A more recent Austrian contribution by Bagus (2009) deepens this subjective theory by introducing the concept of the *utility of money*, understood as the marginal utility derived from money's quality—that is, its perceived capacity to fulfill its functions as a medium of exchange, store-of-value, and unit-of-account. Drawing on Böhm-Bawerk's (1891) idea that the intensity with which individuals value money influences its purchasing power, Bagus proposes that changes in perceived monetary quality shift the position of money on individual value scales. This approach makes money's demand and value directly sensitive to institutional and political factors—such as central bank credibility, legal status, and expected stability—without invoking quantity-based or mechanistic formulations. The "utility of money," in this view, reflects the subjective evaluation of money's *serviceability*, not its consumption, and links changes in its perceived quality to its marginal utility and, ultimately, its purchasing power. Bagus thus revives and extends the Austrian emphasis on subjective valuation by incorporating credibility and quality as endogenous drivers of monetary utility and demand. However, no attempt is done within the Austrian tradition to formalize and operationalize analytically the concept of the utility of money, as SAGE does.

The notion that money could enter directly into a utility function was accepted by mainstream economics only in mid-twentieth century economic thought as a way to model liquidity preference in a tractable fashion. Early work by Samuelson (1947), Patinkin (1965), and Friedman (1969) acknowledged the special role of money in facilitating transactions and hedging against uncertainty, but typically treated this as a background assumption rather than a microfounded mechanism. The formal breakthrough came with Sidrauski (1967), who embedded real money balances into an intertemporal utility function, effectively modeling money as a direct source of satisfaction. This "money-in-the-utility-function" (MIU) approach allowed for stable money demand and monetary policy analysis within a general equilibrium framework.

Despite its analytical convenience, MIU has long been criticized for its ad hoc assumptions. Critics such as Kareken and Wallace (1980) argued that simply inserting money into the utility function lacked theoretical discipline, amounting to a shortcut that ignored the institutional and structural determinants of liquidity. Later critics (e.g., Croushore, 1993) emphasized that money's value derives not from consumption-like utility but from its ability to reduce liquidation costs and facilitate exchange—a budget constraint issue rather than a direct preference.

Efforts to refine MIU included Poterba and Rosenberg (1986), who modeled household preferences over multiple asset types—money, bonds, and equities—each delivering utility based on their distinct liquidity services. Ganchev (2010) later introduced a dynamic marginal utility framework in which the utility of money was linked to its income-generating capacity, proposing that individuals equalize the marginal utility and marginal cost of holding money to maximize welfare.

A parallel literature, originating with Lucas (1978) and developed further by Breeden (1979) in the consumption-based capital asset-pricing model (CCAPM), values financial assets based on their contribution to intertemporal consumption smoothing. In the CCAPM, assets enter indirectly into utility by affecting expected consumption paths and marginal utility over time, and thus provide a rigorous foundation for understanding risk premia and portfolio allocation. However, they do not assign direct utility to holding non-monetary assets.

In fact, while the economic literature has acknowledged the inclusion of money in the utility function—albeit inadequately and incompletely[1]—there has been no notable effort to explore the *direct* utility agents derive from holding non-monetary assets. To address this gap, I proposed in the late 1990s the concept of treating both money and non-monetary assets as competing mechanisms enabling access to real resources across time and states of nature—thus extending beyond the indirect consumption-based valuation of assets methodology.

SAGE builds on this concept, which—unlike earlier MIU and CCAPM formulations—derives the utility of money and other assets from two key dimensions: liquidity (how readily and at what cost an asset can be converted into consumption) and value-storing capacity (how much and how steadily can an asset grow the value stored in it, over time). These dimensions influence an asset's "utility efficiency" and thus shape households' portfolio choices under uncertainty. In this way, SAGE provides a richer, microfounded account of why agents rebalance portfolios as sentiment shifts and liquidity constraints bind.

2.2 Fragmentation across Choice, Finance, and Growth Theory

Modern macroeconomic theory has evolved through distinct and often incompatible traditions. Though these are concerned with intertemporal choice under risk, they typically focus on different actors, mechanisms, and outcomes, and rarely speak the same analytical language.

[1]The existing literature has never explored the origins and nature of the utility that agents extract from the money they hold, let alone provide an analytical derivation of it.

The theory of intertemporal choice is grounded in the Arrow–Debreu (1954) model, which formalized general equilibrium in economies with complete markets and rational agents. Extensions to uncertainty introduced stochastic elements, but the core logic remained focused on consumption and labor supply. Financial assets and capital goods appear only as background constraints or stylized elements of the production function. The representative agent is often treated as a frictionless optimizer, with little attention to liquidity, market incompleteness, or the role of sentiments.

In contrast, financial economics has prioritized asset pricing under risk. The models in this tradition focus on the intertemporal marginal rate of substitution to determine the expected return on risky assets, providing a link between consumption dynamics and financial markets. To better match empirical puzzles such as high equity premia and excess volatility, models introduced features like habit formation (Campbell & Cochrane, 1999), disaster risk (Rietz, 1988; Barro, 2006), or rare shocks. Yet these innovations are typically appended to representative-agent frameworks and assume that asset pricing does not feed back into macroeconomic performance. Moreover, financial assets are often modeled as homogeneous risk bundles, abstracting from their role in liquidity provision under sentiment-contingent (expected) states of the economy.

Growth theory, meanwhile, has traditionally sidelined finance altogether. The Solow (1956) model and its early extensions treated savings as exogenous and investment as a smooth function of aggregate capital. The shift to endogenous growth theory—via Romer (1990), Aghion and Howitt (1998), and others—introduced innovation, knowledge spillovers, and increasing returns, yet largely ignored the financial channels through which investment occurs. Capital accumulation is treated as a technical function, not the result of portfolio decisions under constraints. More importantly, expectations and confidence—which can dramatically affect long-term investment decisions—are almost entirely absent from these models.

SAGE challenges this fragmentation by embedding portfolio allocation at the core of macroeconomic modeling. By integrating households' allocation choices across money, bonds, and productive capital—each with distinct risk and liquidity profiles—SAGE links micro-level preferences with aggregate outcomes like innovation, growth, and macroeconomic volatility. In doing so, it bridges the divide between static utility-maximization frameworks, dynamic asset-pricing models, and long-run growth theory.

2.3 Attempts at Integration

Several literatures have attempted partial integration of these domains, but none have produced a fully unified utility-based framework encompassing choice, finance, and growth. The MIU and cash-in-advance (CIA) models constitute early efforts to link liquidity services to utility or budget constraints. CIA models, such as those developed by Clower (1967) and Lucas and Stokey (1987), impose a constraint that agents must hold money in advance of purchases, capturing liquidity indirectly. While useful for modeling monetary transmission, these approaches rely on exogenous frictions and do not explain how liquidity arises from asset characteristics or sentiment shifts.

The literature on incomplete markets and heterogeneous agents offers richer microfoundations. Bewley (1986), Huggett (1993), and Aiyagari (1994) introduced frameworks in which uninsurable income risk leads to precautionary savings and money demand, producing realistic wealth distributions and consumption dynamics. More recent Heterogeneous Agent New Keynesian (HANK) models (e.g., Kaplan et al., 2018) have shown how portfolio structures affect policy transmission. However, these models are often computationally intensive, tailored to short-run policy analysis, and rarely integrated with growth theory. Moreover, few of them endogenize the formation of sentiment or incorporate it as a state variable influencing asset preferences.

Behavioral economics has contributed insights into how cognitive biases, heuristics, and psychological factors shape decision-making under uncertainty. Foundational work by Kahneman and Tversky (1979) introduced prospect theory, emphasizing loss aversion and reference dependence. Thaler (1990) and Laibson (1997) explored how hyperbolic discounting and present bias distort intertemporal choices. While these models deepen our understanding of deviations from rationality, they often jettison formal optimization and general equilibrium. As a result, they provide limited traction for understanding systemic outcomes like investment cycles or stagnation traps.

Meanwhile, a literature on sentiment and expectations has developed in financial economics and macroeconomic theory. Barberis et al. (1998) modeled investor sentiment as a deviation from Bayesian updating, leading to persistent mispricing and excess volatility. Benhabib and Farmer (1994), Angeletos and La'O (2013), and Lorenzoni (2009) explored how sentiment heterogeneity or self-fulfilling sentiments can generate endogenous business cycles, even without fundamental shocks. Farmer (2013) proposed a "belief function" to replace the traditional Phillips curve, arguing that expectations themselves can anchor multiple equilibria. Yet while these models offer powerful mechanisms for sentiment-driven fluctuations, they do not derive expectations from an underlying utility framework that accounts for asset heterogeneity, liquidity, and structural frictions.

Finally, recursive utility models like those developed by Kreps and Porteus (1978) and Epstein and Zin (1989) have allowed economists to model richer intertemporal preferences, separating risk aversion from intertemporal elasticity of substitution. These have been widely applied in asset pricing and consumption theory. However, they typically assume fixed preferences and rarely integrate sentiment dynamics or liquidity constraints. In particular, they abstract from how sentiments evolve in response to macro-financial developments, and how those evolving sentiments shape portfolio allocations.

SAGE draws together key elements from each of these literatures but reorganizes them within a unified structure. Its innovations are threefold. First, it generalizes utility theory to include assets as differentiated sources of utility, determined by endogenous liquidity and value-storing capacity. Second, it models sentiment as a state-dependent force that influences expectations and behavior without violating rationality. Third, it links asset allocation decisions to long-run outcomes like innovation and growth, enabling a truly integrated macro-financial analysis.

In sum, while prior models have made valuable contributions to understanding parts of the economic system, none has succeeded in unifying the domains of choice, finance, and growth under a single, consistent theoretical umbrella. SAGE is designed to fill this structural gap, offering a framework in which sentiments, liquidity, and portfolio composition are not exogenous constraints or isolated factors, but central, interdependent drivers of economic dynamics.

2.4 Human Reason and Sentiment

A fourth strand of literature crucial to SAGE is the growing body of interdisciplinary research emphasizing the entwinement of reason and sentiment in economic decision-making. While mainstream economics has traditionally assumed that agents form expectations and make choices based on rational optimization alone, a large and expanding literature from behavioral economics, cognitive psychology, and neuroeconomics has revealed that beliefs, emotions, and sentiment play a persistent and structurally important role in shaping economic behavior.

The early critique of the rational expectations hypothesis and the homo economicus model began with Herbert Simon (1955), who introduced the concept of bounded rationality to account for cognitive constraints on information processing. This line of thought was radically extended by Kahneman and Tversky's (1979) development of prospect theory, which showed that preferences are reference-dependent and sensitive to perceived gains and losses—thereby introducing psychological asymmetries into the standard utility framework. Emotions such as fear, hope, and overconfidence were subsequently found to affect choices under uncertainty in ways that could not be reduced to risk preferences or expected utility calculations (Lo, 2004; Shiv et al., 2005).

In macro-financial settings, sentiment has been shown to play a pivotal role in asset pricing, investment decisions, and business cycles. Shiller (2000) demonstrated how irrational exuberance can fuel bubbles disconnected from fundamentals, while Akerlof and Shiller (2009) developed a broader framework of "animal spirits"—capturing the emotional and narrative foundations of consumer and investor behavior. Empirical studies in behavioral finance, such as those by Barberis et al. (1998), showed that investor sentiment can generate persistent deviations from rational pricing, with spillover effects on aggregate outcomes.

From a neuroeconomic perspective, research has identified distinct neural pathways for processing cognitive versus emotional information, but has also found that these systems are deeply integrated in real-world decision-making (Bechara et al., 1997; Camerer et al., 2005). Rather than opposing forces, reason and sentiment are now understood as complementary: emotion helps prioritize, contextualize, and regulate rational choices, particularly under uncertainty.

Affective science and social cognition research offer crucial building blocks for SAGE by demonstrating how emotion-laden beliefs systematically shape economic decision-making under uncertainty. As synthesized in Forgas (2001), affective states are not mere distortions but integral to cognitive processing: they influence how agents attend to information, form judgments, and make intertemporal choices. The Affect Infusion Model discussed therein shows that under complex or uncertain conditions—typical of macro-financial environments—emotions are more likely to infuse judgment, orienting agents' expectations about risk, returns, and the credibility of policy. This aligns with SAGE's premise that prevailing sentiment states—shaped by economic narratives, institutional trust, or collective mood—alter the belief architecture underpinning individual behavior and market dynamics. Rather than treating preferences or beliefs as stable primitives, the social cognition literature provides empirical grounding for SAGE's core claim: that belief formation is, and that shifts in collective affect can endogenously drive macroeconomic fluctuations through cognitive-affective channels.

SAGE incorporates all the above these insights by treating sentiment not as noise or irrationality but as a variable that co-evolves with expectations and market outcomes. Agents respond to changing environments not only through probabilistic inference but also through interpretative mechanisms shaped by mood, confidence, and prevailing narratives. In this respect, SAGE is aligned with Farmer's (2013) emphasis on sentiment-driven equilibria and roots these dynamics within a fully microfounded utility framework that models how shifts in sentiment-contingent rational expectations influence portfolio composition, liquidity preference, and intertemporal trade-offs.

By integrating the literature on reason and sentiment into its theoretical core, SAGE moves beyond the artificial dichotomy between rational and behavioral models. It acknowledges the structural role of sentiment in shaping expectations and actions, and it formalizes this interaction in a way that remains analytically tractable and empirically relevant. This enables a more realistic and encompassing theory of economic behavior—one that reflects how human beings actually navigate uncertainty, make choices, and build the future.

In sum, the growing interdisciplinary literature—from behavioral economics and neuroeconomics to social cognition—has powerfully challenged the notion that economic agents are pure rational optimizers. Empirical evidence now firmly establishes that sentiment and reason are not independent forces, but co-evolving components of decision-making under uncertainty, with direct implications for expectations formation, risk perception, and portfolio behavior.

These interdisciplinary insights motivate the SAGE's treatment of sentiment, reason, and utility as co-evolving primitives of economic agency. While their deeper definition is articulated in Appendix A, Chap. 3 will next offer the theoretical architecture that underpins SAGE's endogenous dynamics and prepares the ground for the formal model presented in Chap. 4.

References

Aghion, P., & Howitt, P. (1998). *Endogenous Growth Theory*. Cambridge, MA: MIT Press.

Aiyagari, S. R. (1994). Uninsured idiosyncratic risk and aggregate saving. *Quarterly Journal of Economics, 109*(3), 659–684.

Akerlof, G. A., & Shiller, R. J. (2009). *Animal spirits: How human psychology drives the economy, and why it matters for global capitalism*. Princeton University Press.

Angeletos, G.-M., & La'O, J. (2013). Sentiments. *Econometrica, 81*(2), 739–779.

Arrow, K. J., & Debreu, G. (1954). Existence of an equilibrium for a competitive economy. *Econometrica, 22*(3), 265–290.

Bagus, P. (2009). The quality of money. *The Quarterly Journal of Austrian Economics, 12*(4), 22–45.

Barberis, N., Shleifer, A., & Vishny, R. (1998). A model of investor sentiment. *Journal of Financial Economics, 49*(3), 307–343.

Barro, R. J. (2006). Rare disasters and asset markets in the twentieth century. *Quarterly Journal of Economics, 121*(3), 823–866.

Bechara, A., Damasio, H., Tranel, D., & Damasio, A. R. (1997). Deciding advantageously before knowing the advantageous strategy. *Science, 275*(5304), 1293–1295.

Benhabib, J., & Farmer, R. A. E. (1994). Indeterminacy and increasing returns. *Journal of Economic Theory, 63*(1), 19–41.

Bewley, T. (1986). Stationary monetary equilibrium with a continuum of independently fluctuating consumers. In W. Hildenbrand & A. Mas-Colell (Eds.), *Contributions to mathematical economics*. North-Holland.

Böhm-Bawerk, E. (1891). *Positive theory of capital*. Translated by William Smart, Macmillan.

Breeden, D. T. (1979). An intertemporal asset pricing model with stochastic consumption and investment opportunities. *Journal of Financial Economics, 7*(3), 265–296.

Camerer, C., Loewenstein, G., & Prelec, D. (2005). Neuroeconomics: How neuroscience can inform economics. *Journal of Economic Literature, 43*(1), 9–64.

Campbell, J. Y., & Cochrane, J. H. (1999). By force of habit: A consumption-based explanation of aggregate stock market behavior. *Journal of Political Economy, 107*(2), 205–251.

Clower, R. W. (1967). A reconsideration of the microfoundations of monetary theory. *Western Economic Journal, 6*(1), 1–9.

Croushore, D. (1993). Money in the utility function: An empirical implementation. *Journal of Money, Credit and Banking, 25*(3), 393–411.

Epstein, L. G., & Zin, S. E. (1989). Substitution, risk aversion, and the temporal behavior of consumption and asset returns. *Econometrica, 57*(4), 937–969.

Farmer, R. E. A. (2013). *The evolution of endogenous business cycles*. MIT Press.

Forgas, J. P. (2001). Introduction: Affect and social cognition. In *Handbook of affect and social cognition* (pp. 1–24). Lawrence Erlbaum Associates.

Friedman, M. (1969). The optimum quantity of money. In *The optimum quantity of money and other essays*. Aldine.

Ganchev, D. (2010). Money-in-the-utility-function models with endogenous liquidity. *Journal of Economic Dynamics and Control, 34*(6), 1072–1084.

Huggett, M. (1993). The risk-free rate in heterogeneous-agent incomplete-insurance economies. *Journal of Economic Dynamics and Control, 17*(5–6), 953–969.

Kahneman, D., & Tversky, A. (1979). Prospect theory: An analysis of decision under risk. *Econometrica, 47*(2), 263–291.

Kaplan, G., Moll, B., & Violante, G. L. (2018). Monetary policy according to HANK. *American Economic Review, 108*(3), 697–743.

Kareken, J., & Wallace, N. (1980). Models of money with spatially separated agents. In *Models of monetary economies*. Federal Reserve Bank of Minneapolis.

Kreps, D. M., & Porteus, E. L. (1978). Temporal resolution of uncertainty and dynamic choice theory. *Econometrica, 46*(1), 185–200.

Laibson, D. (1997). Golden eggs and hyperbolic discounting. *Quarterly Journal of Economics, 112*(2), 443–477.
Lo, A. W. (2004). The adaptive markets hypothesis. *Journal of Portfolio Management, 30*(5), 15–29.
Lorenzoni, G. (2009). A theory of demand shocks. *American Economic Review, 99*(5), 2050–2084.
Lucas, R. E., Jr. (1978). Asset prices in an exchange economy. *Econometrica, 46*(6), 1429–1445.
Lucas, R. E., & Stokey, N. L. (1987). Money and interest in a cash-in-advance economy. *Econometrica, 55*(3), 491–513.
Menger, C. (1892). On the origin of money. *Economic Journal, 2*(6), 239–255.
Mises, L. (1953 [1912]). *The theory of money and credit*. Translated by H.E. Batson. Liberty Fund.
Patinkin, D. (1965). *Money, interest, and prices: An integration of monetary and value theory* (2nd ed.). Harper and Row.
Poterba, J. M., & Rosenberg, J. V. (1986). Testing for heteroskedasticity in asset pricing models. *Journal of Finance, 41*(2), 477–487.
Rietz, T. A. (1988). The equity risk premium: A solution. *Journal of Monetary Economics, 22*(1), 117–131.
Romer, P. M. (1990). Endogenous technological change. *Journal of Political Economy, 98*(5, Part 2), S71–S102.
Samuelson, P. A. (1947). *Foundations of economic analysis*. Harvard University Press.
Shiller, R. J. (2000). *Irrational exuberance*. Princeton University Press.
Shiv, B., Loewenstein, G., Bechara, A., Damasio, H., & Damasio, A. R. (2005). Investment behavior and the negative side of emotion. *Psychological Science, 16*(6), 435–439.
Sidrauski, M. (1967). Rational choice and patterns of growth in a monetary economy. *American Economic Review, 57*(2), 534–544.
Simon, H. A. (1955). A behavioral model of rational choice. *Quarterly Journal of Economics, 69*(1), 99–118.
Solow, R. M. (1956). A contribution to the theory of economic growth. *Quarterly Journal of Economics, 70*(1), 65–94.
Thaler, R. H. (1990). *Quasi Rational Economics*. Russell Sage Foundation.

Chapter 3
The Theory

Contents

Abstract This chapter presents the theoretical structure of SAGE. It constructs a utility function in which agents derive utility not only from consumption and leisure, but also from holding money, bonds, and capital—each evaluated based on liquidity, price volatility, and expected returns shaped by sentiment. The model formalizes the notion of assets as vehicles that enable their holders to carry forward access to real resources across time and states of nature, each with varying "speed" (liquidity) and "power" (store-of-value capacity). It then introduces variable liquidation costs and asset price volatility as endogenous elements shaped by sentiment and the safety and efficiency of financial intermediation. Sentiment is modeled as a state variable that co-evolves with expectations, reflecting the cognitive-affective orientation of agents and influencing how they interpret and act upon information. The economy comprises five sectors—households, firms, financial intermediaries, government, and the central bank—and five markets—goods, labor, money, bonds, and capital. Financial frictions are captured through asset liquidation costs and price volatility. Households allocate wealth intra- and inter-temporally across assets based on their utility. The model produces equilibria where structural fundamentals interact with evolving sentiment to shape macroeconomic outcomes such as employment, inflation, and growth.

B. Bossone, *Bringing Sentiment into Economic Reason*, SpringerBriefs in Economics, https://doi.org/10.1007/978-3-032-08617-4_3

3.1 The Utility of Money and Assets

The function builds upon three blocks: (i) the utility derived by the households from their holding assets, (ii) the costs involved in liquidating assets (including costs of transaction, information, search and matching, etc., and (iii) the households' rational expectations shaped by (changes in) sentiment.

Before discussing these blocks, notice that households order their preferences across consumption C, money M, government bonds B, and shares on productive capital K, according to a strictly quasi-concave, time-separable, and well-behaved utility function $u(\cdot)$, with $u''''(\cdot) > 0$ (that is, decreasing absolute and relative risk aversion). All assets deliver utility to their holders, as discussed below. In this chapter, utility from money and other assets is not just assumed (as it is done in the MIU[1]); it is derived and formalized, and it is used to make assets and consumption all mutually comparable in a general state-dependent equilibrium context driven by optimal microeconomic choices from rational agents (see below). In the utility-based model used here, and as discussed below, asset liquidation costs are variable, and agent expectations are rational but distortable by changes in the state of sentiment that are ultimately driven by changes in economic observables.

In each period, the household earns asset nominal returns $r^n_{a=\in\{M,B,K\}} = (1 + r_a)(1 + p_a)$, where r_a is the real interest rate or the dividend paid on the assets and p_a is the rate of change of asset price P_a. The real rate of return on asset is $r_a = (1 + a)(1 + p^a)(1 - p)$, where p is the economy's rate of inflation. As discussed below, r_a reflects the liquidity and value-storing capacity characterizing each asset, as determined by the market.

Block 1: Assets Provide Utility to their Holders

Asset Utility. Financial assets, from money to tradeable claims on physical (productive) capital, goods, and commodities, are here thought of as "vehicles" that enable their holders to carry forward access to real resources across time and states of nature. Each asset allows its owner to preserve and potentially enhance their capacity to command consumption or productive inputs under uncertainty. The effectiveness of an asset as a vehicle depends on two key characteristics: its "speed," or the time and cost with which it can be mobilized for real purchases (i.e., its liquidity); and its "power," or its ability to store and grow value over time, and protect it against adverse contingencies (i.e., its return and risk profile). In general, greater speed comes at the cost of some power loss, and vice versa. The speed is the greatest for the assets (i.e., monies) that in the exchange process are accepted by all agents, at anytime, anywhere (within the relevant jurisdiction(s)), and at par against all goods, services, and assets traded in the economy—that is, the asset that acts in the economy as means of payment and instrument for settling all (present and future) financial obligations, whether in force of a legal requirement or by societal choice.

[1] See Blanchard and Fischer (1989), Chap. 4.

Capital assets, on the other hand, offer higher power but reduced speed due to illiquidity and volatility.

Because of such property, formalized below, money delivers to its holders a utility margin (or liquidity premium) that all other (less speedy) assets must compensate by paying some extra returns. These extra returns enhance their power as stores of value and, in equilibrium, offset their lower speed. The portfolio composition thus reflects a strategic choice of which vehicles to board, balancing the timing, reliability, and magnitude of future real resource access.

At every instant in time, an asset holder is faced with the likelihood of having to liquidate the asset for her to be able to absorb a consumption shock: changes in likelihood affect differently the utility derived from assets featuring different speeds and power loads. The advantage of a framework where money and assets are "competing vehicles" is that it removes the need for assuming money, exogenously, as "the" asset that can buy commodities (such as under the cash-in-advance, or Clower, constraint), and instead makes money emerge (spontaneously or by design) out of many assets as the one that exchanges against resources within the shortest time interval and at the lowest possible liquidation cost. Notice that money is convertible into real resources or into other assets that are themselves claim on (or convertible into) real resources, implying that its utility derives also from its power to support transactions (e.g., financial transactions) that are not directly related to exchanges against real resources.

The utility of asset a at date t is obtained by summing over two terms: (i) the utility derived from converting the asset into consumption at the next date $t + 1$ with probability ϑ_{t+1}, and (ii) the utility from holding the asset available to access consumption at some later date with residual probability $(1 - \vartheta_{t+1})$. Taking $\mathbf{o}_\tau$ to represent sentiment (to be defined below) at time τ, and calling s_t a shock to consumption at some future date t, for $t > \tau$, the subjective probability of event ϑ_t whereby the asset holder must finance consumption shock s_t is defined as:

$$\vartheta_t \equiv Prob_\tau[(s_{t=\tau+\varepsilon}), \varepsilon \to 0] = \vartheta(\tau_\tau), \vartheta' < 0, \vartheta_t = \begin{cases} \lim\limits_{\mathbf{o}\to\infty} \vartheta(\mathbf{o}_\tau) = 0, \\ \lim\limits_{\mathbf{o}\to 0} \vartheta(\mathbf{o}_\tau) = 1, \end{cases} \text{with } \mathbf{o} \in (0, \infty). \tag{3.1}$$

Equation (3.1) means that the higher the state of pessimism, $\mathbf{o} \longrightarrow 0$, the more asset holders expect consumption shocks to occur in the nearest future, whereas strong optimism leads holders to expect smooth consumption in the near as well as foreseeable future. Indicator Ω is explained below (see Block 3). In the following, $\beta = 1/(1 + \delta)$ is the household's time discount factor, where δ is the household's rate of time preference. For ease of exposition, gross real returns $R_{a\,\in\,\{M,,B,K\}}$ are assumed constant and the price of consumption is set at $P = 1$. Substituting iteratively for $u(a)$ at each forward date yields

$$
\begin{aligned}
u(a_t) &= \beta\{\mathbb{E}_t[u(P_{a_{t+1}}a_t)\vartheta_{t+1}] + u(a_t)(1-\vartheta_{t+1})\} = \beta R_a \mathbb{E}_t[u(P_{a_{t+1}}a_t)\vartheta_{t+1}] \\
&+ \beta^2 R_a^2(1-\vartheta_{t+1})\{E_t[u(P_{a_{t+2}}a_t)\vartheta_{t+2}] + u(a_t)(1-\vartheta_{t+2})\} \\
&= \beta R_a \mathbb{E}_t[u(P_{a_{t+1}}a_t)\vartheta_{t+1}] + \beta^2 R_a^2(1-\vartheta_{t+1})E_t[u(P_{a_{t+1}}a_t)\vartheta_{t+2}] + \beta^3 R_a^3(1-\vartheta_{t+1}) \\
&\times (1-\vartheta_{t+2})\{\mathbb{E}_t[u(P_{a_{t+3}}a_t)\vartheta_{t+3}] + u(a_t)(1-\vartheta_{t+3})\} = \beta R_a \mathbb{E}_t[u(P_{a_{t+1}}a_t)\vartheta_{t+1}] \\
&+ \beta^2 R_a^2(1-\vartheta_{t+1})\mathbb{E}_t[u(P_{a_{t+2}}a_t)\vartheta_{t+2}] + \ldots \beta^i R_a^i(1-\vartheta_{t+1})\ldots(1-\vartheta_{t+i-1}) \\
&\times \{\mathbb{E}_t[u(P_{a_{t+i}}a_t)\vartheta_{t+i}] + u(a_t)(1-\vartheta_{t+i})\},
\end{aligned}
$$

and so on for each subsequent iterative substitution of *u(a)*. Assuming the household consumes all its wealth throughout its time horizon, thereby implying that the holding of any asset a vanishes in the limit since $\lim_{i \to \infty} u(a_t)(1-\vartheta_{t+i}) = 0$, relaxing the constancy of R_a and $P = 1$; considering $\vartheta_t = \vartheta_t(\mathbb{o}_\tau)$, with its dynamics being governed by Eq. (3.1) above, and summing over the household's infinite time horizon, the utility function of asset a at date t can be written in the following general form as

$$
\begin{aligned}
u(a_t) = u(a_t; \mathbb{o}_t) = \mathbb{E}_t \Bigg[\beta R_{a,t+1} \Bigg\{ u\left(\frac{P_{a_{t+1}} a_t}{P_{C,t+1}}\right) \vartheta_{t+1}(\mathbb{o}_t) \\
+ \sum_{\tau=t+1}^{\mathrm{T}=\infty} \beta^\tau \prod_{\tau=t+1}^{T=\infty} u\left(\frac{P_{a_{t+1}a_t}}{P_{C,\tau}}\right) R_{a,\tau}[1-\vartheta_\tau(\mathbb{o}_t)]\vartheta_T(\mathbb{o}_t) \Bigg\} \Bigg],
\end{aligned}
\tag{3.2}
$$

where P_C is the price index of consumer goods. It should be noted that since current and future expectations at any given point in time are conditional on the information available at that time, markets are necessarily incomplete since uncertainty is not eliminable and future probability distributions are subject to shifts that cannot be predicted. In fact, not only probability distributions may shift in unpredictable ways; also, probabilities themselves may be difficult if not impossible for agents to estimate in reality. Yet, what the utility model expressed by Eq. (3.2) allows us to derive, as shown in this book, is how agents change their resource allocation choices as they expect economic conditions to change, giving them more confidence or less to undertake actions with longer-term consequences, even if they cannot calculate future event probabilities with any precision, if at all. In such circumstances, point-estimates of future event probabilities are replaced by future events becoming generically more or less probable, or possible, with higher uncertainty and less confidence being reflected in probabilities ϑ taking large values over more immediate time horizons, or vice versa when the future looks brighter and confidence grows. Knowledge precision is (inevitably) lost to sentiment-contingent rational expectations, which agents use to guide their actions throughout unknown futures, and which they review and update at any point in time, as new news arrive, and new economic conditions materialize.

These features strengthen the support that this model offers to Keynes's liquidity preference theory (LPT) as the foundation to the (intra- and inter-temporal) resource allocation mechanism that underpins the utility-of-money-and-assets theory discussed here. At the same time, this theory offers a powerful way to ground the LPT on microeconomic foundations.

Anticipating Block 3 below, notice that in the hypothetical event of the highest possible level of pessimism ($\omega_t = 0$), the second term on the right-hand side of Eq. (3.2) would equal zero since $\vartheta_{t+1} = 1$ (that is, a_t must be liquidated at $t + 1$ with probability 1), and the utility of a_t would derive from the conversion of the liquidation value of a_t into consumption at date $t + 1$. In the alternative hypothetical event of high optimism ($\Omega' = 1$, see below), the household would not expect to be facing any consumption shock in the immediate or distant future and would then hold a until maturity, when it would either consume its capitalized value or reinvest it into a new asset. In either case, the utility of a_t would derive from converting its future (capitalized) value into consumption at some point in the indefinite future (date T).

Block 2: Variable Asset Value

Liquidation Costs. Every asset a features an optimal "speed," defined as the optimal, or minimum, time-interval $\Delta\tau_a^*$ needed to sell asset a at its market value $(1 - q_a)P_a$, where $q_a^* \in (0, 1)$ is the optimal, or minimum, liquidation unit cost to sell asset a at its market value, consistently with the safety and efficiency (S&E) of financial intermediation.[2] Notice that S&E reflects, more broadly, the quality of the financial system where transactions take place, which involves, inter alia, such features as technology, legal basis, governance, risk management, transparency, market development, market-making capacity, etc.[3] Asset optimal speeds are structural parameters determined by the economy's level of institutional and technological development: all else equal, a more efficient and safe financial infrastructure allows asset liquidation to be effected more rapidly and at lower costs. Asset optional speeds vary depend on the assets' different degree of liquidity: some assets can be liquidated immediately and at very low or no cost; they can thus serve as monies in the exchange system. Liquidating other assets, especially riskier ones, takes longer and involves costs such as for information acquisition; search; analysis, evaluation, and verification; advisory, legal and administrative requirements and services; bargaining and negotiations, etc. Having to liquidate an asset at a higher than its optimal speed (owing, for instance, to immediate and unexpected consumption needs) results in higher liquidation costs or forces the household to accept larger discounts on the asset sale price. Denoting Δt as the time interval available to the asset holder for liquidating asset a, and with a given level of financial infrastructure development, unit liquidation cost q is determined endogenously based on the following conditions:

---

[2]The link between asset liquidation and optimal timing was explored by Lippman and McCall (1986).

[3]For an early and comprehensive discussion of the quality of financial intermediation, see Bossone et al. (2003).

(i) If $0 < \Delta t_a^* < \Delta t$, then $q_a = q_a^* > 0$, that is, the seller has enough time to liquidate a at minimum unit cost;
(ii) If $\Delta t_a^* > \Delta t \geq 0$, then $q_a = q_a^*$, that is, the seller has not enough time and sells a at a unit cost higher than q_a^*,
(iii) As $\lim_{\Delta t^* \geq \Delta t,\, \Delta t \to 0} q_a = 1$, the unit cost of liquidation increases since the time available for the seller to sell a shortens up, and.
(iv) If $\Delta t_a^* = 0$, then $q^* = 0$, that is, a is a perfectly liquid asset (i.e., cash),

where $\Delta t_a^* = \Delta t(\psi, \mathbf{o})$, with $\Delta t'_\psi < 0, \Delta t'_\mathbf{o} < 0$, is the minimum time interval required for the owner of asset a to sell it optimally (i.e., at no loss on its market value). This time interval decreases with the structural variable ψ, which reflects the S&E of financial intermediation, and decreases with $\mathbf{o}$, to be defined below, which captures the sentiment supporting the trading of asset a. Thus, all else equal, greater S&F of the financial infrastructure supporting the market where a is traded, combined with a "seller" market, and strong market optimism, would shorten Δt_a^* and lower liquidation unit cost q^a, and vice versa. Thus, for a given level of S&E, ψ, liquidation unit cost q_a can be written as a function $q_a = q_a(\mathbf{o}) = q\left(\frac{\Delta t_a^*}{\Delta t(\mathbf{o})}\right)$, with $q' > 0$.

Notice that "trust" is a key variable determining the optimal timing for asset trading (that is, the greater the trust, the lower the time interval required for the owner of asset a to sell it optimally).[4] In complex systems characterized by numerous agents who may not know and trust one another, a financial infrastructure with high S&E serves as a "trusted third party" and reduces the costs of asset trading. Market mood interacts with agent expectations and trust in that they speed up transactions (under optimism) and slow them down (under pessimism).[5]

Denote ξ^a the expected utility lost to a's liquidation as a fraction of the expected utility from the consumption financed through the proceeds from the sale of a at date τ,

[4]"Trust" is here defined as the confidence that parties involved in a transaction or interaction will act reliably, ethically, and in good faith. It involves the expectation that each side will fulfill their promises or obligations, without exploitation or deceit, facilitating smooth and cooperative exchanges.

[5]When sentiment is positive (e.g., during economic growth or a bull market), trust in the exchange process increases. Buyers and sellers are more confident in future returns, leading to quicker transactions. For example, during a housing boom, people may rush to buy properties, believing prices will keep rising. In contrast, when sentiment is negative (e.g., during a recession or bear market), trust erodes, and agents become more cautious. This slows down transactions, as buyers fear future losses and sellers worry about falling prices. For instance, during a financial crisis, investors may hesitate to trade stocks, fearing further market declines.

$$\xi_{a_\tau} = \left\{ \frac{\mathbb{E}_t\left[u\left(\frac{q_{a,\tau} P_{a_\tau} a_t}{P_{C,\tau}}\right)\right]}{\mathbb{E}_t\left[u\left(\frac{P_{a_\tau} a_t}{P_{C,\tau}}\right)\right]} \right\} = \xi_a(\mathbb{o}_t), \quad \text{with } \xi' > 0.$$

Then, Eq. (3.2) can then be rewritten as:

$$\begin{aligned} u(a_t) = u(a_t;\mathbb{o}_t) = \mathbb{E}_t[\beta R^a_{t+1}\{u(\frac{P_{a_\tau} a_t}{P_{C,t+1}})\vartheta_{t+1}(\mathbb{o}_t) \\ + \sum_{\tau=t+1}^{T=\infty} \beta^\tau \prod_{\tau=t+1}^{T=\infty} u(\frac{P_{a_\tau} a}{P_{C,\tau+1}}) R_{a_\tau}[1-\vartheta_\tau(\mathbb{o}_t)][1-\xi_{a_\tau}(\mathbb{o}_t)]\vartheta_T(\mathbb{o}_t)\}]. \end{aligned} \tag{3.3}$$

Asset Price Volatility. The asset holder faces the risk that, at any time when the asset needs to be liquidated, she might have to sell it at a loss due to market price volatility. Asset price volatility affects risk-averse agent choices. The utility of each asset, therefore, responds inversely to changes in the expected volatility of the asset price, and Jensen's inequality holds such that,

$$\mathbb{E}_t\left[u\left(\frac{P_{a,\tau} a_t}{P_{C,\tau}}\right)\right] < u\left(\mathbb{E}_t\left[\frac{P_{a,\tau} a_t}{P_{C,\tau}}\right]\right).$$

Call σ^a_τ the ratio of the expected utility loss caused by price volatility to the expected utility from the consumption financed by Q's liquidation at date τ,

$$\sigma_{a_\tau} = \left\{ \frac{\left\{u\left[\mathbb{E}_t\left(\frac{P_{a,\tau} a_t}{P_{C,\tau}}\right)\right] - \mathbb{E}_t\left[u\left(\frac{P_{a,\tau} a_t}{P_{C,\tau}}\right)\right] | \mathbb{o}_t\right\}}{\mathbb{E}_t\left[u\left(\frac{P_{a,\tau} a_t}{P_{C,\tau}}\right)\right]} \right\} = \sigma_a(\mathbb{o}_t), \quad \text{with } \sigma' > 0.$$

Ratio σ^a_τ varies directly with the dispersion of the distribution functions of P^a and P, if they are negatively correlated, and with market pessimism. Equation (3.3) can be further expanded as:

$$\begin{aligned} u(a_t) = u(a_t;\mathbb{o}_t) = \mathbb{E}_t\Bigg[\beta R_{a,t}\Bigg\{u\left(\frac{P_{a,t+1} a_t}{P_{C,t+1}}\right)\vartheta_{t+1}(\mathbb{o}_t) \\ + \sum_{\tau=t+1}^{T=\infty} \beta^\tau \prod_{\tau=t+1}^{T=\infty} u\left(\frac{P_{a,\tau} a_t}{P_{C,\tau}}\right) R_{a,\tau}[1-\vartheta_\tau(\mathbb{o}_t)]\left[1-\xi_{a,\tau}(\mathbb{o}_t)\right][1-\sigma_{a,\tau}(\mathbb{o}_t)]\vartheta_{t+1}(\mathbb{o}_t)\Bigg\}\Bigg], \end{aligned} \tag{3.4}$$

where $u'_a > 0, u'_{P_a} > 0, u'_P < 0, u'_\beta < 0, u'_\theta > 0, u'_\xi < 0, u'_\sigma < 0$.

Equation (3.4) determines the utility of assets across the whole spectrum of liquidity, with variable liquidation costs and price volatility, under rational expectations and changing sentiment shaped by economic observables. In the case of a fully liquid asset (i.e., money), with $\Delta t_a^* = \xi_M^* = \rho_M = 0$, Eq. (3.4) reduces to:

$$
\begin{aligned}
u(M_t) &= u(M_t; \omega_t) \\
&= \mathbb{E}_t \Bigg[\beta(1 - \pi_{t+1}^c) \Bigg\{ u\left(\frac{M_t}{P_{C,\tau}}\right) \vartheta_{t+1}(\omega_t) + \sum_{\tau=t+1}^{\mathrm{T}=\infty} \beta^\tau \prod_{\tau=\mathrm{t}+1}^{T=\infty} u\left(\frac{M_t}{P_{C,\tau}}\right)(1 - \pi_\tau) \\
&\quad [1 - \vartheta_\tau(\omega_t)]\left[1 - \sigma_\tau^M(\omega_t)\right] \vartheta_{t+1}(\omega_t) \Bigg\} \Bigg],
\end{aligned}
$$

that is, as a perfectly liquid asset, money trades against any goods or assets at a sure nominal price, $P_M = 1$, at zero liquidation cost, and bears a zero nominal interest rate.[6,7] Note that the lower the probability of the household having to mobilize liquidity any time soon, the lower the utility derived from holding *M*, and vice versa.

As noted, under heightened optimism the liquidation cost and price variability of illiquid assets could be artificially and temporarily reduced below their minimum values $\xi_a^*, \sigma_a^* > 0$, which should hold under normal conditions for the given financial market structure of the economy considered (see also Chap. 5, footnote 1).

Block 3: Rational Expectations and Sentiment

This block introduces the formal treatment of sentiment and knowledge/information. Their conceptual foundations are discussed in Appendix A.

Expectations Formation. Let $X_\tau = [Y_\tau, \boldsymbol{P}_\tau]$, with $\tau = t + 1, \infty$, where *Y* refers to future income levels and vector ***P*** denotes the vector of future prices of goods and assets. The expected values of the *X* variables coincide with those determined by the model of the economy. At each date, the representative household uses current information set $i_t \in I$ to form and update expectations of the future values of *X*, as a solution of the economy's model. The agent operates transformation $\mathbf{T} : i\mathbf{T} \in (\mathrm{I} \times \mathrm{R}) \rightarrow i \in (0, 1)$, which converts every information bit *i* into a real number Ω drawn from the interval (0,1), reflecting the state of knowledge and information of the agents: as ω moves up (down) along the interval, it reflects a

[6]These features of money may not necessarily hold when people lose trust in it, or in an open-economy context where the domestic currency is traded internationally and may be perceived as an unstable and risky asset. In such case, its liquidation cost and the variability of its shadow price might be non-zero. This point will be discussed in Sect. 4.6.

[7]In economies characterized by advanced financial market infrastructure and government boasting a strong fiscal reputation, short-term (risk-free) government bond *B* tends to be highly traded in liquid monetary markets, featuring low liquidation costs and interest rates. As such, it is often viewed as a viable alternative to money. Conversely, longer-term bonds, corporate bonds, and equities exhibit lower liquidity levels, incur higher liquidation costs, are subject to increased risks and price fluctuations, and consequently demand higher return premiums to entice investor participation. Holding all other factors constant, a surge in pessimistic expectations diminishes the appeal of more liquid assets (and conversely enhances it for optimistic expectations), thus influencing their demand and the equilibrium rates of return. This approach broadens the scope of the framework initially proposed by Giovannini (1989).

higher (lower) level of knowledge and information about the economy, and hence more (less) precise expectations about of the future values of X, which the agent extracts from the information set available and processes through her accumulated knowledge of the economy. At each date t, the evolution of the agent's expectations of the future values of X is governed by the following distribution function:

$$F_t(X_T|\Omega_t) = \sum_{n=1}^{N|\Omega} (w_{n,T}|\Omega_t) F_{t,n}(X_T), T > t, \tag{3.5}$$

where $w_T : 0 \leq w_{n,T} \leq 1; \sum_n w_{n,T} = 1$, and where the weights w's and the order N of the set of selected distribution functions are conditional on state of knowledge and information Ω_t. Equation (3.5) associates a specific structure of weights to N different probability distribution functions of X. A "high" value of state variable Ω, reflecting strong knowledge and good information, implies a small set (i.e., a small N) of narrowly dispersed distribution functions of X, each with a large w_T attached, leading to more precise predictions of future X's: in the limit case of $\Omega_t = 1$ (that is, perfect knowledge and full information), then $N = 1$ and $w_T = 1$, such that $F_t(X_T| 1) = F_t(X_T)$. On the other hand, a low value of Ω, reflecting poor knowledge and limited information, implies a broad set (i.e., a large N) of dispersed distribution functions, each with a small w_T attached: no single distribution dominates the others in the agent's expectations, and each has a very low probability of being the "true" one. In "fan-chart" diagram terms, the band would be very large and all predicted values within it would have the same shadings since none would have a higher likelihood than the others. In the extreme case of a value of ω very proximate to 0, then $w_{nT} \cong 0, \forall n$, and the distribution $F_t(X_T)$ would be indeterminate (the width of the fan-chart band would be infinite).

Sentiment. Agent expectations are affected by (changes in) sentiment, that is, the mood about the state of the world, which prevails in the environment where the agents operate and interacts with their information and knowledge on the state of the economy.[8] Also the reverse is true, whereby expectations about the future affects current sentiment. The latter ranges between (a maximum level of) "optimism" and (a minimum level of) "pessimism": Optimism (pessimism) is the state of mind inducing an agent to expect superior (inferior) outcomes of future events than would be reasonable for the agent to anticipate on the exclusive basis of the knowledge and the information available to her. Formally, expectations are said to be "optimistic" when,

[8]For a recent empirical analysis of how market moods translate into narratives and affect the macroeconomic performance, see Flynn and Sastry (2024).

$$\mathbb{E}_t\left[X_T|\Omega_t'\right] \succ \mathbb{E}_t[X_T|\Omega_t] \text{ or } \mathcal{W}_t\left(\mathbb{E}_t\left[X_T|\Omega_t'\right]\right) > \mathcal{W}_t(\mathbb{E}_t[X_T|\Omega_t]), \text{for } T > t \text{ and } \Omega_t' > \Omega_t,$$

where $\mathcal{W}$ is the welfare associated with the expected value of X, and the reverse sign holds in both expressions for "pessimistic" expectations, and where the *perceived* state of the world Ω' is the result of information orientational or directional process $\mathbb{O} \ni \{\mathbb{o}_t\}_{t=0}^{\infty} : \mathbb{O} \in (I \times R) \rightarrow \Omega' > \Omega$ for $\Omega < 1$, *or* $\Omega' < \Omega$ for $\Omega > 0$, with Ω', $\Omega \in (0, 1)$, whereby $\mathbb{o}_t = \frac{\Omega_t'}{\Omega_t} \in (0, \infty)$ is the sentiment indicator introduced earlier, which measures the outcome of the continuous interplay between sentiment and reason based on information and knowledge, such that: (i) $\mathbb{o}_t \rightarrow 0$, implying $\Omega_t' = 0$, signals extremely high pessimism; (ii) $\mathbb{o}_t \rightarrow \infty$, with $\Omega_t' \gg 0$ and $\Omega \approx 0$, signals extremely high optimism; and (iii) $\mathbb{o}_t = 1$, implying $\Omega_t' = \Omega$, marks the boundary between optimism and pessimism and reflects the rational expectations-consistent benchmark value of indicator $\mathbb{o}$.[9]

At each date, through $\mathbb{o}_t$, sentiment process $\mathbb{O}$ orientates the expected value of the variables that are relevant to the agent, to an extent that depends on the intensity of the prevailing emotions, much as individuals experience in their real-life situations when they see the very same contingency under a different light depending on the underlying state of their mind, often under the influence of the prevailing social context. This process can be understood as the product of individuals' "animal spirits" as these may be socially influenced by agents observing each other's moods and behaviors and by their own psychological attitudes. At the same time, changes in expectations may feed back into sentiment and alter individual and collective perceptions and attitudes.

Optimism (pessimism), therefore, orientate the way agents process and interpret the information available to them, and, as knowledge progresses, better information becomes available, and new feedback are received from the observed reality, agents adjust their sentiment possibly causing their "orientated" (optimistic or pessimistic) expectations to converge (though not necessarily linearly) toward their "unorientated" equivalent, implying convergence of $\mathbb{o}_t$ toward its benchmark value of 1. The special feature of this model is that it incorporates uncertainty and sentiment as separate and interacting dimensions of the economy, which affect expectations formation, and vice versa. Their interaction is captured by Chart 3.1 under deliberately extreme assumptions.

The combinations reported in the chart clarify the relationship between the two state variables Ω and Ω' and their different economic interpretations. An agent can have very pessimistic and yet very accurate expectations about the future, if she has

[9] Specifically, $\mathbb{o}_t = 1$ defines a sentiment-neutral benchmark in which agents interpret the available information and knowledge without distortion, so that expectations remain unbiased in the directional sense—neither more optimistic nor more pessimistic than warranted—reflecting a state where market mood does not skew perceptions, sentiment does not interfere with information processing, and any deviation from perfect foresight stems solely from informational incompleteness rather than sentiment-influenced reinterpretation.

Chart 3.1 Combinations of state variables concerning uncertainty and sentiment and behavioral responses (under extreme assumptions)

Values of Ω (information/knowledge) Values of Ω' (sentiment)	Very low	Very high
Very low	$\Omega' \cong \Omega \cong 0 : o \approx 0$ Strong pessimism High uncertainty $\Rightarrow$ Indefinite expectations of extremely bad outcomes $\Rightarrow$ Fear, wait and see, inaction	$0 \cong \Omega' < \Omega \cong 1 : o \approx 0$ Strong pessimism Quasi certainty $\Rightarrow$ Definite (accurate) expectations of extremely bad outcomes $\Rightarrow$ Informed self-protective action
Very high	$1 \cong \Omega' > \Omega \cong 0 : o \rightarrow \infty$ Strong optimism High uncertainty $\Rightarrow$ Indefinite expectations of extremely good outcomes $\Rightarrow$ Prone to positive action	$\Omega' \cong \Omega \cong 1 : o \rightarrow 1$ Strong optimism Quasi certainty $\Rightarrow$ Definite (accurate) expectations of extremely good outcomes $\Rightarrow$ Fully calculable positive action taking

enough knowledge and information to back them up, or she can have very optimistic and yet very uncertain expectations due to not having enough knowledge and information.

The interactions between Ω and Ω' may run deeper, since the information and knowledge used by the agents affect their sentiment, the latter in turn may influence the information that agents select and the way they used their knowledge base. These interactions, however, will not be further explored in this book and might well be a topic for future research (see Chap. 6).

Sentiment and the Economic Environment. Sentiment responds to the evolving economic environment. While changes in sentiment necessarily reflect subjective, psychological processes of individual human beings and the mechanisms governing their social interactions, this chapter assumes that they are nonetheless influenced by the observation of reality as filtered through knowledge (Frydman & Goldberg, 2011). Among the factors that drive changes in sentiment critical are: (a) the perceptions of general economic (in)stability; (b) the performance of relevant markets; and (c) relevant news, innovations, and forecasts. Through simple indicators, it can be shown how these three classes of factors influence sentiment (see Appendix B). The relevance of the indicators does not lie in their specific form, but in that they reflect the notion whereby agent emotions are not unexplained "sunspots" and derive, instead, from the ongoing interactions of human states of mind with information, knowledge, and rationality and their influence on agent responses to real circumstances.

A Methodological Note on Covariances, Asset Pricing, and SAGE's Utility Structure
A question may arise as to why the SAGE framework, unlike the CCAPM, does not derive asset valuations from their covariance with marginal utility of consumption. The answer lies in the model's foundational structure. SAGE assigns direct, state-contingent utility to money and non-monetary financial assets—reflecting agents' subjective assessments of liquidity, trust, volatility, and access to resources across time and states of nature. This departs from CCAPM, where assets matter only insofar as they smooth consumption. In SAGE, preference shifts across portfolio components are driven by evolving sentiment-contingent utility factors, not by second-order covariance effects. These utility factors capture dynamic adjustments to perceived risk, liquidity, and price volatility—the very variables that covariances proxy for in traditional models. Thus, covariance behavior can emerge in SAGE endogenously as a by-product of shifting preferences and sentiment-contingent dynamics, without needing to be modeled explicitly. This allows SAGE to model environments where sentiment and liquidity dynamics dominate observed behavior, that is, in contexts where standard covariance-based pricing falls short.

3.2 The Economy's Model

This section presents the structure of SAGE model using a general equilibrium framework. Building on the generalized utility-based valuation of market items (e.g., commodities, goods, services, labor, money, and financial and nonfinancial assets), the model features an economy with five sectors: a representative household, a representative firm, the financial sector, the government, and the central bank, and five markets: for goods, labor, money, credit, government bonds, and productive capital.

Households
At each time *t*, households supply labor services L_t to firms at nominal wage w_t and derive utility from both using their income $w_t L_t$ to consume and to accumulate wealth by purchasing assets, and from leisure. Households chooses L_t to equate the marginal disutility of labor with the marginal value of real wages, conditioned on expectations. Their disutility from work increases with hours and is modeled as convex to capture effort costs. Households use their non-consumed income and may also borrow extra money M_{CR} from the financial sector at interest rate r_{CR} to invest into various types of assets ranging from zero-interest bearing money holdings M, to government bonds B paying interest r_B, and equity shares issued by firms against productive capital K and returning rate r_K. By purchasing equity shares, households finance firms' accumulation of K.

The representative household derives utility from every (money and non-money) asset it holds, according to the general function illustrated in Sect. 3.1. Using the reduced-form of this function (derived in Appendix C), the household's overall utility function is:

$$U(C_t, M_t, B_t, K_t, L_t; \text{©}_t) = log\, C_t + \theta_M(\text{©}_t)\, log\left(\frac{M_t}{P_{C,t}C_t}\right)$$

$$+ \theta_B(\text{©}_t)\, log\left(\frac{P_{B,t}B_t}{P_{C,t}C_t\left[1 + \xi_{B,t}(\text{©}_t) + \sigma_{B,t}(\text{©}_t)\right]}\right)$$

$$+ \theta_K(\text{©}_t)\, log\left(\frac{P_{K,t}K_t}{P_{C,t}C_t\left[1 + \xi_{K,t}(\text{©}_t) + \sigma_{K,t}(\text{©}_t)\right]}\right) - \chi\frac{L_t^{1-\nu}(\text{©}_t)}{1+\nu}, \tag{3.6}$$

where utility is additive and separable across arguments, for analytical tractability, and is conditional on sentiment ©_t defined in Sect. 3.1; C is consumption; M is money; B is government bond; K is productive capital; P_C is the price of consumption bundle; P_B and P_K are the market prices of bond B and capital K, respectively; $\theta_a(\text{©}_t) \geq 0$, $\in(M, B, K)$, are preference weights for holding money, bonds, and capital, respectively—they reflect how much utility the agent assigns to holding each asset relative to others, depending on agent expectations shaped by sentiment (see also below); $\chi > 0$ and $\nu \geq 0$ are labor disutility parameters; the ratios $\frac{P_{a,t}a_t}{P_{C,t}C_t}$ represent relative wealth allocations; and the term $\frac{1}{1+\xi_{a,t}(\text{©}_t)+\sigma_{a,t}(\text{©}_t)}$ is an efficiency discount factor that takes into account variable asset liquidation costs $\xi_{a,\ t}$ and the volatility of asset-market prices $\sigma_{a,\ t}$, conditional on sentiment ©_t, as discussed in Sect. 3.1. Notice that $\xi_{K,\ t} > \xi_{B,\ t}$ and $\sigma_{K,\ t} > \sigma_{B,\ t}$, $\forall\ t$. In the case of money ($a = M$), $\xi_{M,\ t} = 0$, and $\sigma_{M,\ t} = 0$, $\forall\ t$, since money is fully liquid and its nominal price never changes.[10]

Special emphasis deserves the role of weights $\theta_a(\text{©}_t)$'s (see also Appendix D). Each weight encodes an equilibrium object—the marginal rate of substitution between the utility from asset a and consumption, conditional on sentiment. Eq. (6) collapses the forward-looking problem reflected within the original general asset utility Eq. (3.4) into a sentiment-contingent reduced-form representation, where $\theta_a(\text{©}_t)$ captures the endogenous equilibrium utility weight the representative household assigns to asset a, contingent on sentiment ©_t.

It is fundamentally important to notice that finance enters SAGE through the intra- and inter-temporal portfolio choices that households make, based on the utility they (expect to) derive from all the resources available to them (i.e., consumption, labor, money, and all sorts of financial and non-financial assets they can access in their respective markets).

The utility-maximizing household evaluates its future income perspectives $y_t's$, $\forall t$, by considering its expected job value JV as affected by sentiment ©_t:

[10] As noted, these features of money may not hold when people lose trust in it, either domestically or internationally when it trades against other currencies. This point will be discussed in Sect. 4.6.

$$\mathbb{E}_t[y_\tau|\mathbb{o}_t] = \mathbb{E}_t\left[y_\tau^{\{[JV_\tau(\mathbb{o}_t)/\overline{\Pi}]\}}\right], \tag{3.7}$$

defined in Appendix E, where: $JV_t(\mathbb{o}_t) = \mathbb{E}_t\left[\sum_{\tau=t+1}^{\infty}\prod_{i=t}^{\tau}\beta_i(p_\tau x_\tau - w_t)|\mathbb{o}_t\right]$; x is the household's output; $\overline{\Pi}$ is the normal rate of firms' profit; β is the time discount factor; $\mathbb{E}_t[\ldots|\mathbb{o}_t]$ is the operator of rational expectations conditional on (shaped by) sentiment—the job value declines with pessimistic prospects about future levels of remuneration and risk of unemployment, and vice versa under optimistic prospects).[11]

The household's dynamic optimization problem is thus:

$$\underset{\{C_t, M_t, B_t, K_t, L_t\}}{\text{Max}} \mathbb{E}_0\left[\sum_{t=0}^{\infty}\beta^t U(C_t, L_t, M_t, B_t, K_t; \mathbb{o}_t)\right], \tag{3.8}$$

subject to the intertemporal budget constraint:

$$P_{C,t}C_t \leq M_t + \Delta M_{H,t} + P_{B,t}B_t + P_{K,t}K_t + \mathbb{E}_0\sum_{t=0}^{\infty}\mathbb{E}_t[y_t|\mathbb{o}_t]$$
$$+ r^n_{B,t-1}P_{B_{t-1}}B_{t-1} + r^n_{K,t-1}P_{K,t-1}K_{t-1} + M_{t-1} - r^n_{M,t-1}\Delta M_{H,t-1}, \tag{3.9}$$

and to transversality condition

$$\lim_{t\to\infty}\beta^t\mathbb{E}_0[M_t + P_{B,t}B_t + P_{K,t}K_t] = 0. \tag{3.10}$$

Equation (3.9) holds for a class of otherwise homogeneous households and ΔM_H is the money that some of them borrow from others, or lend to others and to firms, with $\Delta \gtreqless 0$ for each household, correspondingly, at nominal interest rate r^n_M, through financial intermediation (see below). In Eq. (3.10), the present value of financial and capital assets vanishes in the limit, ensuring that the household eventually consumes its wealth rather than hoarding or endlessly borrowing or lending.

The household chooses a portfolio that balances the utility from present and future consumption and from assets with different liquidity and value-storing capacity, which change over time based on rational expectations shaped by sentiment. In the OLG extension of SAGE (see Sect. 4.13), household expectations are governed by a sentiment-contingent rational-expectations kernel that evolves with generational sentiment and historical experience.

[11] Specifically, $\frac{JV_t}{\overline{\Pi}} = 1$ holds under normal economic conditions and $\frac{JV_t}{\overline{\Pi}} > 1$ (< 1) under optimistic (pessimistic) expectations.

Firms

Firms produce output Y_t by employing labor services from households at current wage w_t and using productive capital K_t, whose stock accumulates periodically according to $K_t = I_t + (I - d)K_{t-1}$, where d is the rate of capital depletion and I is innovative (technology augmenting) investment. In each period, the representative firm finances production by borrowing $\Delta M_{F,\ t}$ at nominal interest rate $r^n_{M,t}$ from households through financial intermediation (see below), and finances investment by issuing equity shares that are absorbed by the households' non-consumed portion of income allocated to it, $I_t = W_tL_t - (M_t - M_{t-1}) - (B_t - B_{t-1})$, based on relative risk-return considerations across the spectrum of assets available. Firms distribute capital return r_K to the households. Firms maximize profits over their (infinite) time horizon:

$$\begin{aligned}\underset{K_{t-1},L_t}{\text{Max}}\ \Pi_t = P_{Y,t}Y_t + \Delta M_{F,t-1} - W_tL_t - r^n_{K,t-1}P_{K,t-1}K_{t-1}\\ - r^n_{M,t-1}\Delta M_{F,t-1},\end{aligned} \tag{3.11}$$

where P is the output price and W is nominal wage, subject to the standard Cobb-Douglas production function:

$$Y_t = A_tK_t^{\alpha}L_t^{1-\alpha}, \tag{3.12}$$

where total factor productivity A_t is endogenous and follows the following process:

$$A_{t+1} = A_t(1+\phi_I I_t), \quad \text{with } I_t = k\frac{K_t}{1+\xi_{K,t}(\mathbb{o}_t)+\sigma_{K,t}(\mathbb{o}_t)}, \tag{3.13}$$

where ϕ_I measures how effectively innovation-related investment I translates into productivity growth; k is the share of productive capital K_t that is directed to innovative investment I—it can be thought of as a structural intensity parameter for innovation within capital accumulation: a higher η_K means that for a given capital stock, more is devoted to growth-enhancing use;[12] $\sigma^2_{I_{t+1}}$ is the market price volatility of capital K; and the term $\frac{1}{1+\xi_{K_t}(\mathbb{o}_t)+\sigma_{K_t}(\mathbb{o}_t)}$ is the innovation efficiency discount factor, which captures how frictions and perceived uncertainty reduce the effective portion of capital allocated to productivity-enhancing innovation, based on agent expectations as influenced by sentiment.

Financial Intermediation

Financial intermediation is here imagined as a fully decentralized and agentless public network utility that facilitates households' borrowing money ΔM_H from

---

[12]For completeness, one could distinguish between a share of capital that is invested in traditional (not technology augmenting) and a (complementary) share that is investment in innovative forms of capital. This distinction is omitted here for simplicity.

other households at interest rate r_M^n, and lending it to other households and/or to firms at the same interest rate.[13]

Although no banks or other intermediaries are formally represented in the model, the critical effects of financial intermediation on the economy are subsumed by the central role that two key financial variables—liquidation costs and asset prices volatility—play in the determination of the asset values, and hence the allocation choices of the agents. Both variables change in response to changes in agents' sentiment-contingent rational expectations and to changes in the quality of financial intermediation (defined in Sect. 3.1).

Subject to monetary policy decisions from the central bank (see below), money creation for financing purposes is allowed in the model, which enables agents to borrow money to expand current consumption or investment choices.

The financial intermediation function represented in the model acts as a veil that mirrors the agents' allocation choices and investment decisions, without influencing or interfering with them. This minimalistic approach is adopted to keep the model simple and yet make it capable to incorporate (variable) financial frictions and to analyze their impact on the macroeconomy. Integrating the explicit role of financial intermediaries in the model, however, would be crucial to study the amplification effects that they have on the economy in response to shocks originating within and/or outside of the financial sector, as noted in Sect. 4.5.and Chap. 6.

Government

The government produces a non-pecuniary public good G and finances its production by issuing bond B and setting taxes T,

$$G_\tau + r_{B_{t-1}} P_{t-1}^T B_{t-1} = P_{B_t} B_t + T_t, \tag{3.14}$$

under transversality condition:

$$\lim_{T\to\infty}\left(\prod_{\tau=t}^{T-1}\frac{1}{1+r_{B,\tau}}\right) P_{B,T} B_T = 0, \tag{3.15}$$

which ensures that the present value of government debt converges to zero and fiscal policy remains solvent in the long run.

The government sells as many bonds B as households wish to buy at their market price. The functional form of the household demand for B can be written in the simple general form:

$$B_t = B\big(P_{B,t}, P_t, P_{K,t} \text{ with } B_B' < 0,\ \ B_P' > 0, B_K' > 0. \tag{3.16}$$

[13]Notice that for the households that lend money to the financial sector, the terms ΔCR_t and $r_{CR} M_{CR,\,t-1}$ would enter Eq. (3.4) with negative and positive sign, respectively.

Notice that since G is a non-pecuniary public good, it is not sold in the market, it does not generate income for, or transfers to, households or firms, and therefore it does not contribute directly to output (i.e., domestic GDP), that is, it is not a marketed output exchanged for a price.

Central Bank
The supply of M responds to the central bank's policy rule:

$$M_t = M_{CB} + M_{CR} = M\left(r^n_{B,t} - r^{n*}\right), \quad \text{with } M' > 0 \text{ if } r^n_{B,t} - r^{n*} > 0, \tag{3.17}$$

where $r^n = r + p$. According to rule (3.17), the central bank governs the supply of M, consisting of base money M_{CB} and credit money M_{CR}: the former is issued against the purchase of bonds B, and the latter is loaned to financial intermediaries for further lending to the households. It is assumed that the central bank keeps $r_{CR,\,t} = r_{B,\,t}$.

Through rule (3.17), the central bank seeks to minimize deviations over time between the nominal interest rate on (short-term and risk-less) treasury bond B and the neutral nominal rate of interest r^{n*} that holds when real-sector supply and demand are in intertemporal equilibrium and inflation is constant (earlier it was assumed that $p = 0$).

The role of such policy rule is more important than it may at first appear. Given the essentially neutral role of the financial sector, as described above, the central bank's policy rule (3.17) enables the money supply to grow endogenously in response to household portfolio demand—provided this expansion does not generate inflation. This endogeneity introduces greater flexibility into asset markets, as further discussed in Chap. 4.

3.3 General Equilibria

The equilibrium of this economy, conditional on sentiment, is a sequence of allocations and prices $\{(C_t, L_t, M_t, B_t, K_t, w_t, p_t, r_{B,t}, r_{K,t})|\mathfrak{o}_t\}_{t=0}^{\infty}$, such that households maximize utility given expectations and budget constraint; firms maximize profits; all markets clear; and expectations evolve based on the market-sentiment factor $\mathfrak{o}_t$.

Setting $P = 1$, using it as numéraire, and solving model (3.1)–(3.17) for the first-order conditions with respect to C_t, L_t, M_t, B_t, K_t give the general equilibrium quantities, prices, and returns reported in Chart 3.2, where the shorter notation $\Delta\mathcal{E}a_t(\mathfrak{o}_t) \equiv 1 + \xi_{a,t}(\mathfrak{o}_t) + \sigma_{a,t}(\mathfrak{o}_t)$, for $a \in \{M, B, K\}$, with $\frac{\partial \mathcal{E}a_t}{\partial \mathfrak{o}_t} < 0$, is introduced for convenience.

At the heart of this equilibrium configuration is the liquidity-efficiency valuation of assets. Notice that the intra-temporal equilibrium solution in Chart 3.2 does not reflect a financial arbitrage condition, but a utility-based indifference condition. Households optimize utility across the spectrum of available assets, under the

Chart 3.2 Solutions to SAGE model

Variable Market	Quantity	Price	Gross return
Goods	$P_y Y_t = P_{C,\ t} C_t + P_{K,\ t} I_t$		
Labor	$L_t = \left(\frac{\lambda_t w_t}{\chi}\right)^{\frac{1}{\nu}} = \left(\frac{(1-\alpha) A_t K_t^{\alpha}}{w_t}\right)^{\frac{1}{\alpha}}$	$w_t = \frac{\chi}{\lambda_t} L_t^{\nu}$	
Money	$M_t = \frac{\theta_M(\mathbb{o}_t) P_{C,t} C_t}{\lambda_t P_{M,t}}$	Nominal price $P_{M,\ t} = 1$ Shadow price $\mathcal{P}_{M,t} = \frac{\theta_M(\mathbb{o}_t) P_{C,t} C_t}{\lambda_t M_t}$	Nominal return $R_{M_t} = 1$ Shadow return $\mathcal{R}_{M_t} = \frac{1}{\mathcal{P}_{M,t}} = \frac{\lambda_t M_t}{\theta_M(\mathbb{o}_t) P_{C,t} C_t}$
Bond	$B_t = \frac{\theta_B(\mathbb{o}_t) P_{C,t} C_t \Delta\mathcal{E}^2_{B_t}(\mathbb{o}_t)}{\lambda_t P_{B,t}}$	$P_{B,t} = \frac{\theta_B(\mathbb{o}_t) P_{C,t} C_t \Delta\mathcal{E}^2_{B,t}(\mathbb{o}_t)}{\lambda_t B_t}$	$R_{B,t} = \frac{1}{\Delta\mathcal{E}^2_{B,t}(\mathbb{o}_t)}$
Capital	$K_t = \frac{\theta_K(\mathbb{o}_t) P_{C,t} C_t \Delta\mathcal{E}^2_{K_t}(\mathbb{o}_t)}{\lambda_t P_{K,t}}$	$P_{K,t} = \frac{\theta_K(\mathbb{o}_t) P_{C,t} C_t \Delta\mathcal{E}^2_{K,t}(\mathbb{o}_t)}{\lambda_t K_t}$	$R_{K,t} \frac{1 + r_{K,t} - \delta}{\Delta\mathcal{E}^2_{K,t}(\mathbb{o}_t)}$
Memo	$\lambda_t = \frac{1 - \theta_M(\mathbb{o}_t) - \theta_B(\mathbb{o}_t) - \theta_K(\mathbb{o}_t)}{C_t}$ $\Delta\mathcal{E}a_t(\mathbb{o}_t) = 1 + \xi_{a,t}(\mathbb{o}_t) + \sigma_{a,t}(\mathbb{o}_t)$		
Optimal allocations			
Intra-temporal	$\frac{\lambda_t}{P_{C,t} C_t} = \frac{\theta_a(\mathbb{o}_t)}{P_{a,t} B_t \Delta\mathcal{E}^2_{B,t}(\mathbb{o}_t)}$ for $a \in \{M, B, K\}$		
Inter-temporal	$1 = \beta \mathbb{E}_t \left[\frac{U_C(c_{t+1})}{U_C(C_t)} R^a_{t+1}\right]$ for $a \in \{M, B, K\}$		

constraint that each asset carries a gross efficiency discount factor $\Delta\mathcal{E}_{a,t}(\mathbb{o}_t) = 1 + \xi_{a,t}(\mathbb{o}_t) + \sigma_{a,t}(\mathbb{o}_t)$. In pessimistic sentiment states, both the perceived illiquidity and the expected price volatility rise, reducing the utility-based marginal valuation of illiquid assets, particularly capital. Households respond by reallocating wealth toward safer, more liquid stores, notably money and government bonds. Vice versa for optimistic sentiment states. Thus, under SAGE, multiple equilibria may arise, depending on the evolution of expectations shaped by (changing) sentiment.

References

Blanchard, O. J., & Fischer, S. (1989). *Lectures on Macroeconomics*. Cambridge, MA: MIT Press.

Bossone, B., Mahajan, S., & Zahir, F. (2003, January). *Financial infrastructure, group interests, and capital accumulation: Theory, evidence, and policy*. IMF Working Paper No. 03/24.

Flynn, J. P., & Sastry, K. (2024). *Narratives about the macroeconomy*. NBER Working Paper No. W32602.

Frydman, R., & Goldberg, N. (2011). *Beyond mechanical markets: Asset price swings, risk, and the role of the state*. Princeton University Press.

Giovannini, A. (1989). Uncertainty and liquidity. *Journal of Monetary Economics, 23*(2), 239–258.

Lippman, S. A., & McCall, J. J. (1986). An Operational Measure of Liquidity. *American Economic Review, 76*(1): 43–55.

Chapter 4
Applications

Contents

Abstract This chapter demonstrates the flexibility and explanatory power of SAGE by applying it to a range of relevant macroeconomic phenomena. It shows how boom–bust cycles, secular stagnation, and asset bubbles emerge as sentiment-contingent equilibria, even in the absence of structural shocks. The equity premium puzzle is explained by the disutility of illiquid, volatile capital, while exchange rate overshooting arises from rational portfolio shifts under belief swings. Sudden stops and capital flow reversals are traced to sentiment-induced liquidity preference shifts among global investors. The chapter also explores how financial frictions—such as liquidation costs and weak intermediation—amplify these dynamics by altering asset utility and portfolio composition. Growth is shown to depend not only on capital accumulation but also on sentiment-driven innovation incentives and financial structure. Labor force participation is modeled as a function of the perceived value of work, shaped by expectations of future returns and job security under varying sentiment regimes. Inflation dynamics are reinterpreted through shifts in liquidity preference and confidence, which can suppress or accelerate price pressures. SAGE is finally extended to an overlapping generations structure, allowing for demographic heterogeneity, intergenerational sentiment propagation, and life-cycle

B. Bossone, *Bringing Sentiment into Economic Reason*, SpringerBriefs in Economics, https://doi.org/10.1007/978-3-032-08617-4_4

portfolio behavior. Collectively, these applications illustrate how SAGE replicates real-world dynamics as rational outcomes under uncertainty and belief asymmetry, offering a unified framework for analyzing diverse macro-financial phenomena.

In this chapter, SAGE is applied to show how it contributes to explain such diverse and important economic phenomena—specifically, (i) booms and bust dynamics, (ii), secular stagnation, (iii) the equity premium puzzle, (iv) exchange rate overshooting, (v) financial frictions, (vi) sudden stops and capital reversals, vii) global portfolio asymmetries, (viii) drivers of growth, endogenous growth, and sentiment-driven long-run growth; (ix) labor participation, and (x) inflation regimes—using rational household choices shaped by sentiment. SAGE is also (xi) extended to an overlapping generations (OLG) structure, allowing for demographic heterogeneity, intergenerational sentiment propagation, and life-cycle portfolio behavior.

4.1 Booms and Busts

Boom–bust cycles emerge endogenously in SAGE as rational equilibrium responses to fluctuations in sentiment $\mathbb{o}_t \epsilon R$, which governs the formation of expectations through four key mechanisms, depending on how it affects: (i) the perceived probability $\vartheta(\mathbb{o}_t)$ of immediate liquidity needs; (ii) the cost of asset liquidation $\xi_{K,\ t}$; (iii) the volatility of future asset returns or prices $\sigma_{K,\ t}$; and (iv) job value $JV_t(\mathbb{o}_t)$. These mechanisms shape the representative household's intra- and inter-temporal portfolio allocation and labor supply decisions, discussed in Chap. 3.

Recurrent boom–bust cycles typically unfold within a bounded range of optimistic-pessimistic sentiments, implying mean reversion of the sentiment dynamics, which ensures that expectations fluctuate but do not collapse or shoots sky-high uncontrollably.

Define a cyclical domain $\mathbb{O}^{cycle} = \{\mathbb{o}_t : \mathbb{o}_L < \mathbb{o}_t < \mathbb{o}_U\}$, where L and U stand, respectively, for lower and upper, whereby sentiment dynamics remain bounded and reversible. Within $\mathbb{O}^{cycle}$, sentiment $\mathbb{o}_t$ is assumed to evolve according to a bounded stochastic process of the kind $\mathbb{o}_t = Prob(\mathbb{o}_{t-1}, \varepsilon_t)$ where ε_t is a noise term. More realistically, $\mathbb{o}_t$ can also jump based on observed or perceived changes in the state of the world. As long as $\mathbb{o}_t \in\ \mathbb{O}^{cycle}$, cycles are bounded and reversible. Section 4.2 addresses dynamics beyond $\mathbb{O}^{cycle}$.

As in Sect. 3.2, households allocate wealth across current consumption, money, bonds, and capital. The demand for capital is $K_t = \frac{\theta_K}{\lambda_t P_{K,t} \Delta \mathcal{E}^2_{K,t}(\mathbb{o}_t)}$. Within $\mathbb{O}^{cycle}$, an increase in optimism $\mathbb{o}_t$ reduces future asset liquidation cost $\xi_{K,\ t}$ and price volatility $\sigma_{K,\ t}$ relative to other assets, thereby lowering the efficiency discount factor of capital $\mathcal{E}_{K_t}(\mathbb{o}_t)$ more than for other assets. Consequently, the demand for capital K_t rises relative to the other assets.

Since $\frac{\partial K_t}{\partial \Delta \mathcal{E}_{K,t}} = -\frac{2\theta_K}{\lambda_t P_{K,t} \Delta \mathcal{E}_{K,t}^2} < 0$ and $\frac{\partial^2 K_t}{\Delta \mathcal{E}_{K,t}^2} = \frac{6\theta_K}{\lambda_t P_{K,t} \Delta \mathcal{E}_{K,t}^4} > 0$, capital demand reacts convexly to sentiment shifts. Thus, small increases in optimism yield large increases in capital accumulation when initial sentiment is near the upper level of pessimism (and vice versa). The rise in K_t increases investment, which fuels endogenous innovation and productivity growth via $A_{t+1} = A_t(1 + \phi I_t)$ (see Sect. 4.7). Higher capital also raises expected returns $r_{K,t} = \frac{\alpha A_t \left(\frac{K_t}{L_t}\right)^{\alpha-1}}{P_{K,t}}$,[1] and strengthens job value $JV_t(\mathbb{o}_t)$ through both higher wages and lower expected disutility from work, reinforcing optimism.

A surge in sentiment increases the marginal utility of capital relative to other competing assets its rational benchmark. This generates **market incentive**:

$$\mathcal{M}\left(K_t, P_t^K; \mathbb{o}_t\right) = -\theta_K \log\left(\frac{\Delta \mathcal{E}_{K,t} \mid \mathbb{o}_t \neq 1}{\Delta \mathcal{E}_{K,t} \mid \mathbb{o}_t = 1}\right),$$

where as discussed in Sect. 3.1, Sentiment $\mathbb{o}_t = 1$ is the rational-expectations-consistent benchmark. Market incentive $\mathcal{M}$ is positive (negative) when $\mathbb{o}_t > (<)\ 1$. In the former case, both capital allocation and its price rise beyond the rational-expectations-consistent benchmarks. Moreover, $\forall \mathbb{o}_t$ such that $\lim_{t<t^*} \mathbb{o}_t = +\infty$, over investment time horizon $t \in [t_0, t^*)$, where t^* is the time limit within which shares of K can be sold at no loss, feeds **bubble:**

$$\mathcal{B}(K_t, P_{K,t}; \mathbb{o}_t) = \left\{(K_t, P_{K,t}) | \mathbb{o}_t > 1 \gg \left(K_t^*, P_{K,t}^*\right) | \mathbb{o}_t = 1\right\}.$$

This state is characterized by over-extended portfolios and inflated capital asset prices. This is because during the given time-interval investors rush to buy K and keep doing so due to overoptimistic expectations. The reverse holds for $\mathbb{o}_t < 1$, where $\mathcal{M} \ll 0$. Here, $\mathbb{o}_t$ causes bust $\mathcal{B} \ll 0$ if $\lim_{t<t^*} \mathbb{o}_t = 0$, where t^* is the time after which shares of K can be re-entered (re-purchased) at no loss, reflecting the unwinding of pessimism-driven discounts. This is because during the given time-interval investors fire-sale K and keep doing so due to very pessimistic expectations.

The dynamics analyzed above, which lead to $\mathcal{M}, \mathcal{B} \gg 0$, explain the seemingly paradoxical situations in which both asset stocks and prices rise simultaneously, as discussed by Phelps (2009) in relation to the housing sector.[2] The magnitudes of $\mathcal{M}$

[1]The return on capital r_{K_t} rises despite the likely increase in in P_K. This occurs because: $\frac{K_t}{L_t}$ increases, raising the marginal productivity of capital; A_t increases due to larger innovative investment; and P_K rises, as it reflects higher future returns and lower risk premia, but not enough to offset the decline in the numerator. The partial derivatives reveal this effect, $\frac{\partial r_{K_t}}{\partial K_t} = \frac{\alpha(\alpha-1)A_t\left(\frac{K_t}{L_t}\right)^{\alpha-2}}{P_{K,t}} < 0$ and $\frac{\partial r_{K,t}}{\partial A_t} > 0$.

[2]Phelps, cit., addressed this apparent paradox—a rising stock of an asset (like housing) driving up rather than down its price—by focusing on expectations of future returns and the role of perceived profitability in sustaining demand. In Phelps's explanation, when people expect continued capital gains from an asset, rising supply does not necessarily lead to falling prices. Instead, if the demand

and $\mathcal{B}$, together, provide a metric of the market's "irrational exuberance"—which is not that irrational, after all.

Following the expansion phase, as K_t accumulates, diminishing returns at some point set in, since $\frac{\partial r_{K,t}}{\partial K_t} = \frac{\alpha(\alpha-1)A_t}{P_{K,t}L_t^2} K_t^{\alpha-2} < 0$ as $\alpha - 1 < 0$ in Cobb-Douglas. As the increase in capital valuation P_K outpaces productivity gains, and starts being perceived as overvaluation, the direction of sentiment reverses and households start expecting a rise in both capital liquidation cost and price volatility, since $\frac{\partial \xi_{K,t}}{\partial(\mathbb{o}_t)}, \frac{\partial \sigma_{K_t}}{\partial(\mathbb{o}_t)} < 0$, thereby triggering disinvestment. This generates a feedback loop where overextension breeds financial fragility. The economy hits a turning point as sentiment reverts due to diminishing returns and/or narrative corrections, leading to a sentiment contraction within $\mathbb{O}^{cycle}$. A fall in $\mathbb{o}_t \in \mathbb{O}^{cycle}$, then, reverses the expansion: the contraction in investment and innovation lowers productivity and wages. To the extent that $\mathbb{o}_t \in \mathbb{O}^{cycle}$, however, spontaneous recovery is possible if the recession is seen as opening opportunities for new investment. The downturn is thus a bust, not a trap (see below).

The stylized boom–bust episodes discussed in this section can be further illuminated by examining how financial cycles emerge endogenously in SAGE from sentiment-driven portfolio dynamics. Box 4.1 formalizes these mechanisms and explores their long-run consequences.

Box 4.1 Financial Cycles as Sentiment-Driven Dynamic Processes

Financial cycles are characterized by expansions and contractions in credit, asset prices, and risk appetite that often exceed the variation in underlying fundamentals. In SAGE, these cycles emerge endogenously from the co-evolution of sentiment and rational expectations, and are reinforced through feedback loops involving liquidity, volatility, and intra–/inter-temporal utility from asset holdings.

Boom–bust transitions through portfolio shifts

Optimistic sentiment raises the expected utility of illiquid, high-return assets (notably productive capital), leading households to reallocate wealth

(continued)

is driven by speculative or optimistic expectations, the growing stock can reinforce those expectations. This creates a self-fulfilling dynamic: as more housing is built and sold at higher prices, the public interprets this as evidence of strong and persistent returns, which boosts demand further and supports even higher prices. This can occur especially in an environment of low interest rates or loose credit, where access to financing magnifies speculative behavior. Phelps highlighted how macroeconomic disequilibria—such as persistent excess liquidity or distorted perceptions of risk—can drive such paradoxical dynamics, leading to housing booms and busts. This insight helps explain how bubbles form: rising asset prices attract more demand, which should, under standard supply-demand reasoning, reduce prices—instead, it fuels further price increases because of momentum-driven expectations and sentiment-contingent demand.

Box 4.1 (continued)
toward them. This shift compresses liquidity premia and inflates asset prices, stimulating investment and growth while reinforcing the optimistic outlook.

However, this capital-intensive allocation increases systemic vulnerability. When sentiment declines (i.e., $\mathbb{O}_t$ declines), agents reassess the utility of illiquid assets in light of expected consumption shocks and tighter liquidity constraints. A flight to liquidity ensues: capital is sold off in favor of money or liquid bonds, asset prices fall, investment collapses, and pessimistic expectations are validated. The resulting bust is thus a sentiment-contingent equilibrium switch, not necessarily triggered by exogenous shocks. These sentiment-contingent reallocation dynamics are consistent with the view of endogenous cycles emphasized by Farmer (2012) and resemble leverage-driven boom–bust transitions as described in Geanakoplos (2010).

Amplification and persistence through sentiment-contingent frictions

The key to the persistence of financial cycles in SAGE lies in the fact that financial frictions themselves—Liquidation costs and price volatility—Are functions of sentiment. A decline in s raises both the expected costs of liquidating assets and their price uncertainty, reducing their utility just when liquidity is most needed. This generates a self-reinforcing loop: Sentiment decline ⇒ higher liquidation cost and price variability of less liquid assets ⇒ lower utility of less liquid assets ⇒ portfolio retrenchment ⇒ prices of less liquid assets decline, and financial instability rises ⇒ sentiment declines further.

These dynamics are formalized in this section via the gross efficiency discount factor $\Delta\mathcal{E}_{K,t}(\mathbb{O}_t) = 1 + \xi_{K,t}(\mathbb{O}_t) + \sigma_{K,t}(\mathbb{O}_t)$, which penalizes illiquid and volatile assets more severely in pessimistic states. The bust may become abrupt if sentiment crosses a critical threshold, beyond which agents anticipate immediate liquidity needs and rush to exit illiquid positions—a mechanism conceptually related to the sentiment-contingent stagnation traps discussed in sect. 4.2.

The amplification process modeled here echoes the financial accelerator mechanisms proposed by Brunnermeier and Sannikov (2014), in which endogenous risk and balance sheet dynamics reinforce macroeconomic volatility.

Growth hysteresis and long-term effects

The effects of financial cycles go beyond temporary dislocations. They reshape the long-term growth path via:

- **Path dependence in capital accumulation**: Booms can stimulate investment and innovation, raising the effective capital stock and pushing the economy onto a higher growth path. However, if followed by sharp busts, the destruction of capital values and collapse in risk appetite can lock the

(continued)

Box 4.1 (continued)

economy into a lower-growth equilibrium. This mechanism directly links to Sect. 4.8 on the drivers of growth.

- **Sentiment-dependent utility weights**: In pessimistic states, households assign lower marginal utility to future consumption, reducing the incentive to invest in long-horizon, productive capital. This underinvestment equilibrium aligns with Sect. 4.9 on endogenous growth under liquidity and portfolio constraints, where growth is driven by investment flows shaped by portfolio utility.
- **Sentiment-contingent stagnation traps**: If pessimistic sentiment persists, even with unchanged fundamentals, the economy may become trapped in a self-reinforcing low-growth equilibrium. This connects to Sect. 4.10 on sentiment and long-run growth, where expectations and narrative dynamics shape the trajectory of capital formation and innovation.

Thus, financial cycles in SAGE are not merely cyclical—They are structural, with the potential to anchor or derail long-run growth trajectories depending on the path and persistence of sentiment.

Relation to capital flow dynamics

These same mechanisms extend to the open-economy context, as analyzed in Sect. 4.6 on sudden stops and capital flow reversals for an application to cross-border portfolio reallocations. When domestic sentiment deteriorates, capital flows outward in search of liquidity and institutional safety, triggering balance-of-payments pressures and external adjustment needs.

These boom–bust patterns are not anomalies but inherent features of a utility-maximizing framework where rationality and sentiment (inherently) interplay. The dynamics emerge endogenously from the above-described feedback loop from sentiment to asset liquidity, portfolio reallocations, changes to real variables, and back to sentiment—a loop where each term amplifies or dampens the next. As long as $\omega_t > \omega^C$ and policies are adopted to keep it there, this loop supports bounded, nonlinear oscillations in capital, productivity, wages, and job value. In this case, boom–bust cycles are possible to the extent that the sentiment process unfolds but remains above the threshold $\omega_t \geq \omega_L > \omega^C \Longrightarrow \exists \mathbb{E}_t[\omega_{t+n}] > \omega_t, \forall n$.

Conversely, traps can materialize if sentiment drops at or below a critical threshold ω^C, where dynamics become non-mean-reversing. In this case, the economy enters a "secular stagnation" regime, analyzed in the next section, where optimism cannot recover spontaneously to push the economy out of the trap and into a better equilibrium.

4.2 Secular Stagnation

The existence of critical sentiment threshold $\mathbb{o}^C$ introduces a nonlinear bifurcation in the dynamics of the economy, bearing important implications. This threshold demarcates the boundary between cyclical behavior, on one hand, where expectations self-correct, and stagnation behavior, on the other, where pessimistic beliefs become self-reinforcing. The dynamics of capital demand and sentiment are no longer symmetric across $\mathbb{o}^C$, giving rise to a sentiment-induced stagnation trap. The existence of such threshold is illustrated in Appendix F.

Let the household's marginal utility of capital be:

$$U_K \mid \mathbb{o}_t = \frac{\omega_K}{\Delta \mathcal{E}_{K,t} \mid \mathbb{o}_t},$$

where $\omega_K \equiv \theta_K \frac{P_{K,t}}{P_{C,t}}$ is the normalized utility weight per unit of wealth, and $\frac{\partial \Delta \mathcal{E}_K}{\partial \mathbb{o}} < 0$, and $\frac{\partial^2 \Delta \mathcal{E}_K}{\partial \mathbb{o}^2} > 0$.[3] The demand for capital is therefore given by:

$$K_t^D \vert \mathbb{o}_t = \frac{\omega_K}{\lambda_t \; \Delta \mathcal{E}_{K,t}(\mathbb{o}_t)}.$$

Hence, the demand for capital is strictly increasing and convex in $\Delta \mathcal{E}_{K,t}$, and thus strictly decreasing and concave in $\mathbb{o}_t$.

At threshold $\mathbb{o}^C$, the household is indifferent between holding capital and switching to liquid assets, such that:

$$U_K \mid \mathbb{o}^C = U_M \mid \mathbb{o}^C.$$

Then, for any $\mathbb{o}_t > \mathbb{o}^C$, the housheld holds capital, while for any $\mathbb{o}_t \leq \mathbb{o}^C$, capital is dominated by other (less liquid) assets.

Because $\mathcal{E}_{K,t}(\mathbb{o}_t)$ is convex, the response of the demand for capital to sentiment exhibits a downward asymmetry:

$$\lim_{\mathbb{o}_t \to \mathbb{o}^{*-}} \left| \frac{\partial K_t^D}{\partial \mathbb{o}_t} \right| \gg \lim_{\mathbb{o}_t \to \mathbb{o}^{*+}} \left| \frac{\partial K_t^D}{\partial \mathbb{o}_t} \right|. \tag{4.1}$$

Inequality (4.1) captures the asymmetry in recovery and collapse dynamics around the threshold. It says that as sentiment deteriorates below $\mathbb{o}^C$, the rate at

[3] This new expression for the marginal utility of capital is derived from Eq. (3.6) in Sect. 3.2 where $U_K \mid \mathbb{o}_t = \theta_K(\mathbb{o}_t) \log\left(\frac{P_{K,t} K_t}{P_{C,t} \Delta \mathcal{E}_{K,t}(\mathbb{o}_t)}\right) = \log(\omega_t) - \log(\Delta \mathcal{E}_{K,t}(\mathbb{o}_t))$, and dropping the logarithmic transformation for a tractable measure of effective utility, so that $U_K \mid \mathbb{o}_t = \frac{\omega_t}{\Delta \mathcal{E}_{K,t}}$.

which capital demand K_t collapses is much steeper than the rate at which capital demand recovers when sentiment improves and crosses the threshold from above.[4]

When sentiment deteriorates below $\mathbb{o}^C$, the economy transitions from a domain of self-correcting boom–bust cycles $\mathbb{O}^{cycle} = \{\mathbb{o}_t : \mathbb{o}_t > \mathbb{o}^C\}$ into a structurally distinct regime of persistent underperformance $\mathbb{O}^{stag} = \{\mathbb{o}_t : \mathbb{o}_t \leq \mathbb{o}^C\}$. In this stagnation regime, expectations do not recover endogenously: instead, portfolio choices, innovation, and income dynamics become self-reinforcing in the direction of contraction.

Importantly, the transition to stagnation is hysteretic. Due to the convexity of $\Delta\mathcal{E}_{K,t}(\mathbb{o}_t)$, when sentiment states $\mathbb{o}_t$ deteriorate beyond critical threshold $\mathbb{o}^C$, the economy transitions from the cyclical domain $\mathbb{O}^{cycle}$ into a structurally distinct regime characterized by persistent underperformance. In the post-threshold regime $\mathbb{O}^{stag}$, the sentiment dynamics do not support recovery: the endogenous feedback mechanisms that allow boom–bust cycles to self-correct now become self-reinforcing in the opposite direction. In other words, in this stagnation regime, expectations do not recover endogenously: instead, portfolio choices, innovation, and income dynamics become self-reinforcing in the direction of contraction.

In stagnation regime $\mathbb{O}^{stag}$, the reduction in $r_{K,\ t}$ and the decline in JV_t feed into each other to a much greater degree than within the cyclical domain $\mathbb{O}^{cycle}$: as the marginal utility of money (and other liquid assets) rises relative to capital, the equilibrium drifts toward a configuration of high savings in liquid assets, low investment, and stagnating productivity and output. Even if temporary, pessimism may cause permanent stagnation.

The Jacobian matrix governing the dynamics of $(K^C, \mathbb{o}^C)$ sets the conditions for local (in)stability. Specifically:

$$\mathcal{J} = \begin{bmatrix} \dfrac{\partial K_{t+1}}{\partial K_t} & \dfrac{\partial K_{t+1}}{\partial \mathbb{o}_t} \\ \dfrac{\partial \mathbb{o}_{t+1}}{\partial K_t} & \dfrac{\partial \mathbb{o}_{t+1}}{\partial \mathbb{o}_t} \end{bmatrix}, \text{with } \det(\mathcal{J}) > 1 \Longrightarrow \text{unstable saddle} - \text{path dynamics.}$$

Economically, condition $\det(\mathcal{J}) > 1$ signals that the mutual feedback between capital and sentiment is strong enough to destabilize the system—rising optimism fuels investment, which in turn reinforces optimism, leading to self-reinforcing boom–bust dynamics (see Appendix G for a derivation of the condition). In this case, the stagnation equilibrium is both suboptimal and resilient to marginal shocks: suboptimal since there exist Pareto-superior equilibria (with higher capital, output, and utility), but the economy is stuck in a self-consistent low-welfare trap; resilient to marginal shocks since the stagnation equilibrium absorbs or neutralizes small

[4]Mathematically, the separating role of the critical sentiment threshold $\mathbb{o}^S$ could be formalized using piecewise-defined functions, regime-switching dynamics, and derivative discontinuities or convexity shifts, which would all signal that once sentiment crosses $\mathbb{o}^S$, behavior changes fundamentally—e.g., from reversible to self-reinforcing dynamics, or from smooth to sharply nonlinear capital reallocation.

shocks, implying that recovery requires coordinated or large-scale expectation shifts.[5]

This mechanism generates a liquidity-dominant, low-output equilibrium—an endogenous liquidity trap in utility space—without requiring nominal interest rates to fall to the zero lower bound. Even with accommodative monetary conditions, households prefer to hold liquidity not for transaction purposes but for intertemporal insurance, reflecting the irreducible value of safety when sentiment collapses. This recursive mechanism creates a self-sustaining stagnation trap.

The stylized stagnation dynamics in SAGE resonate with observed episodes such as Japan's lost decades (1990s–2020s) and the Eurozone's post-2008 malaise, where high liquidity preference persisted despite extremely low interest rates. In both cases, households and firms exhibited durable pessimism, redirecting wealth into safe assets and suppressing investment. These patterns are consistent with SAGE's prediction that a fall in $ɷ$ below $ɷ^C$ results in an endogenously persistent, sentiment-driven stagnation.

The stagnation regime derived in SAGE departs significantly from traditional models of secular stagnation (e.g., Summers, 2014; Eggertsson & Mehrotra, 2014), which typically invoke exogenous structural drags (e.g., demographics, savings gluts, or a binding zero lower bound). By contrast, SAGE shows that stagnation is an endogenous utility-optimization equilibrium under preferences. Notably, the liquidity trap arises in utility space—i.e., from rising marginal utility of liquid assets—not in interest rate space. This reframes stagnation as a preference-consistent asset allocation under endogenous pessimism.

Notice that the existence of a critical sentiment threshold $ɷ^C$ is not imposed exogenously, but emerges endogenously from the structure of utility-maximizing behavior. Under standard convexity and monotonicity assumptions on $\Delta\mathcal{E}_{K,t}(ɷ_t)$ and the utility of liquidity, there exists a unique $ɷ^C \in (0, 1)$ at which the economy tips from a capital-accumulating regime into a **stagnation trap**. This threshold marks the point of sentiment-induced behavioral bifurcation.

4.3 The Equity Premium Puzzle

The equity premium puzzle (Mehra & Prescott, 1985) refers to the empirical fact that the average return on equities exceeds that on government bonds by a much larger margin than can be justified by standard intertemporal models of consumption smoothing under expected utility.

For instance, the CCAPM framework cannot account for the observed magnitude of the equity premium without assuming either extreme risk aversion or implausibly

[5] A thorough (utility-based) analysis and evaluation of the policy tools available to push the economy out of secular stagnation is presented in Bossone (2025), Chap. 12, "Money and Secular Stagnation," pp. 287–318.

volatile consumption. In general, the conventional explanations fail to account for the possibility that assets themselves, rather than consumption alone, may differ systematically in their utility-delivering capacity, especially when beliefs about liquidity and volatility are endogenous. SAGE departs from this view by shifting attention from intertemporal consumption smoothing to differences in asset utility, which can explain high premia under moderate, realistic behavioral assumptions.

Within SAGE, the puzzle is not a paradox but an equilibrium outcome of rational portfolio allocation under utility efficiency. As discussed in Sect. 3.1, under SAGE, the representative household derives utility not only from consumption and leisure but also from holding assets of various nature, each delivering a flow of utility proportional to its efficiency-adjusted, intra- and inter-temporal consumption value.

Letting the household choose asset allocations (B_t, K_t) to maximize lifetime utility according to the optimal program discussed in Chap. 3, the Euler equations for bonds and capital are, respectively:

$$1 = \beta \mathbb{E}_t \left[\frac{1}{C_{t+1}} r_{B_{t+1}} \frac{1}{1 + \xi_{K,t+1}(\mathbb{o}_t) + \sigma_{K,t+1}(\mathbb{o}_t)} \right]$$

and

$$1 = \beta \mathbb{E}_t \left[\frac{1}{C_{t+1}} r_{K,t+1} \frac{1}{1 + \xi_{K,t+1}(\mathbb{o}_t) + \sigma_{K,t+1}(\mathbb{o}_t)} \right].$$

Subtracting these two conditions, letting $\pi_K \mid \mathbb{o}_t = \{(\mathbb{E}_t[r_{K,t+1}] - \mathbb{E}_t[r_{B,t+1}]) | \mathbb{o}_t\}$ be the equity premium determined by sentiment-contingent rational expectations, and rearranging, yield the SAGE-based expression:

$$\mathbb{E}_t \left[\frac{1}{C_{t+1}} \pi_K \frac{1}{1 + \xi_{K,t+1}(\mathbb{o}_t) + \sigma_{K,t+1}(\mathbb{o}_t)} \right] = \mathbb{E}_t \left[\frac{1}{C_{t+1}} r_{B_{t+1}} \frac{(\xi_{K,t} + \sigma_{K,t}) - (\xi_{B,t} + \sigma_{B,t})}{1 + \xi_{K,t+1}(\mathbb{o}_t) + \sigma_{K,t+1}(\mathbb{o}_t)} \right]. \tag{4.2}$$

The decomposition in the RHS of expression (4.2) reveals the utility efficiency differential as the key force driving the equilibrium equity premium, that is the difference in utility losses. This differential is formally grounded in the utility function derived in Sect. 3.2, where the asset-specific efficiency discount factor reflects both the asset's expected liquidation cost and price volatility. The latter depend not only on the asset's liquidity characteristics but also on the agents' sentiment-contingent rational expectations about future conditions. The utility efficiency of capital falls nonlinearly in $\mathbb{o}_t$, due to the denominator structure of the efficiency discount factor $\frac{1}{1+\xi_{K,t+1}(\mathbb{o}_t)+\sigma_{K,t+1}(\mathbb{o}_t)}$. This generates convex utility losses in response to linear increases in pessimism. Even in the absence of large consumption shocks, the relative inefficiency of capital (due to higher $\xi_{K,t} + \sigma_{K,t}$) necessitates a higher expected return.

In SAGE, the equity premium arises not merely from risk aversion, but from differences in the perceived usefulness of assets as vehicles to future consumption, especially under uncertainty. Capital assets such as equity are less liquid and have more volatile prices than government bonds, making them less effective in supporting future consumption. This gap in utility efficiency is amplified by pessimistic beliefs, which increase households' concerns about asset liquidity and valuation risk. As a result, in downturns or fragile environments, capital must offer significantly higher returns to remain attractive in household portfolios. SAGE model thus rationalizes a large, time-varying equity premium as an equilibrium response to utility differences—not as an anomaly.

Furthermore, because asset liquidation cost ξ and price variability σ vary with sentiment ϖ, SAGE predicts not just a persistent equity premium, but also time variation in its magnitude. In particular, when sentiment volatility rises—say, in cases of heightened uncertainty—households perceive greater fragility in the utility of capital. This increases the required premium for holding equity, generating equity premia that are countercyclical and heteroskedastic.

This perspective aligns with empirical evidence (Lettau & Ludvigson, 2001): equity premia are observed to spike during recessions and financial crises, when investors shift away from riskier assets despite often small consumption shocks. SAGE captures this pattern by showing that pessimistic expectations amplify the perceived disutility of capital through utility efficiency losses—driving return differentials even in the absence of large shocks or rare disasters.

SAGE therefore reinterprets the equity premium as an equilibrium reflection of sentiment-contingent preferences—providing a microfounded explanation for time-varying premia and portfolio shifts, and offering a unified framework for analyzing financial instability and systemic risk under rational expectations.

The above formalism allows to reinterpret the equity premium as the price of utility-based asset valuation, with the following implications:

(i) **Countercyclical premia:** when sentiment deteriorates, the disutility penalty on capital increases disproportionately. Since $\xi_{K,t} + \sigma_{K,t} > \xi_{B,t} + \sigma_{B,t}$, the wedge between the utility-based returns of capital and bonds widens. Households demand a larger premium to hold capital—consistent with observed countercyclical equity premia in data.

(ii) **Endogenous flight to safety**: even modest shifts in ϖ_t can sharply reduce the utility of capital, prompting households to reallocate toward money and bonds. This flight to safety behavior does not require rare disasters or preference non-separability—it follows from standard optimization under sentiment-adjusted asset utilities.

(iii) **No need for exotic preferences:** SAGE does not require recursive utility, rare disaster risk, or other modifications to the utility function over consumption. Instead, it re-specifies how assets enter the utility function, thereby delivering observed return premia, using familiar functional forms and rational expectations.

To conclude, whereas conventional models (such as the CCAPM or recursive utility models) struggle to explain sudden spikes in the equity premium without invoking large consumption shocks, extreme risk aversion, or rare disasters, SAGE accounts for them as natural outcomes of shifts in sentiment. In SAGE, even modest deteriorations in sentiment—say, an increase in pessimism—sharply degrade the utility efficiency of capital due to nonlinear penalties on liquidity and price volatility. This generates discontinuous jumps in the required return on equity—closely mirroring empirical observations during crises. The model thus offers a more behaviorally plausible and analytically tractable explanation for sharp, episodic increases in equity premia.

4.4 Exchange Rate Overshooting

SAGE also rationalizes the phenomenon of exchange rate overshooting, where exchange rates respond more strongly in the short run than in the long run to shocks such as monetary expansions, as an outcome of portfolio rebalancing driven by agents' utility preferences. To show this result, let us extend the model to a small open-economy setting where domestic households can hold both domestic and foreign assets. Let then the household choose holding money M, domestic bonds B_D, foreign bonds B_F, and capital K. Foreign bonds are denominated in foreign currency, with the nominal exchange rate e_t defined as the domestic currency price of one unit of foreign currency. The household now maximizes a utility function of the form:

$$U = \sum_{t=0}^{\infty} \beta^t u(C_t, L_t M_t, B_{Dt}, e_t B_{F,t}, K_t; \omega_t)$$

subject to:

$$P_{C,t}C_t + P_{B_D,t}B_{D,t} + e_t P_{B_F,t}B_{F,t} + \mathrm{P}_{K,t}K \leq w_t L_t + M_t + \Delta M_{H,} + r^n_{B_D,t-1}P_{B_D,t}B_{D,t-1}$$
$$+ e_t r^n_{B_F,t-1}P_{B_F,t-1}B_{F,t-1} + r^n_{K,t-1}P_{K,t-1}K_{t-1} - r^n_{M,t-1}\Delta M_{H,t-1}$$

Let r_{B_D} and r_{B_F} denote the real interest rates on domestic and foreign bonds, respectively. The first-order conditions for domestic and foreign bond holdings yield, respectively:

$$\frac{1}{\Delta\mathcal{E}_{B_D,t}(\mathbb{o}_t)}\frac{1}{1+r_{B_D,t}}=\beta\mathbb{E}_t\left[\frac{u'_C(C_{t+1})}{u'_C(C_t)}\frac{P_{C,t}}{P_{C,t+1}}|\mathbb{o}_t\right]$$

and

$$\frac{1}{\Delta\mathcal{E}_{B_F,t}(\mathbb{o}_t)}\frac{e_t}{(1+r_{B_F,t})\mathbb{E}_t[e_{t+1}|\mathbb{o}_t]}=\beta\mathbb{E}_t\left[\frac{u'_C(C_{t+1})}{u'_C(C_t)}\frac{P_{C,t}}{P_{C,t+1}}|\mathbb{o}_t\right].$$

Rearranging yields the sentiment-adjusted uncovered interest parity (UIP) condition:

$$r_{B_D,t}-r_{B_F,t}=\mathbb{E}_t\left[\frac{\Delta e_{t+1}}{e_t}|\mathbb{o}_t\right]+\log\left(\frac{\Delta\mathcal{E}_{B_D,t}(\mathbb{o}_t)}{\Delta\mathcal{E}_{B_F,t}(\mathbb{o}_t)}\right).$$

The term $\pi_e\,|\,\mathbb{o}_t=\log\left(\frac{\Delta\mathcal{E}_{B_D,t}(\mathbb{o}_t)}{\Delta\mathcal{E}_{B_F,t}(\mathbb{o}_t)}\right)$ represents the sentiment-contingent, rational-expectations exchange rate risk premium. When $\mathbb{o}_t$ declines, this premium increases if foreign assets are perceived to be more liquid or stable than domestic ones—pushing the exchange rate further above its long-run equilibrium.

Suppose the domestic central bank initiates a monetary expansion that lowers $r_{B_D,t}$. Under standard UIP, this would cause a depreciation of e_t to offset the interest differential. In the SAGE model, however, if markets perceive the country's overall policy framework to be poorly credible,[6] the monetary shock may trigger a downward shift in sentiment, $\mathbb{o}_t$, reflecting increased uncertainty. If households view domestic bonds as less safe or liquid than foreign ones, i.e., $\xi_{B_D,t}+\sigma_{B_D,t}>\xi_{B_F,t}+\sigma_{B_F,t}$, then $\pi_e\,|\,\mathbb{o}_t=\log\left(\frac{\Delta\mathcal{E}_{B_D,t}(\mathbb{o}_t)}{\Delta\mathcal{E}_{B_F,t}(\mathbb{o}_t)}\right)>0$. The households demand a larger depreciation today (i.e., a higher e_t) for them to be induced to hold domestic bonds despite their inferior utility-based returns. The exchange rate must thus overshoot its long-run equilibrium $\overline{e}$ to equilibrate utility-based returns:

$$e_t>\overline{e}=\lim_{t\to\infty}e_t.$$

The degree of overshooting $\widehat{e}_t$ depends directly on the sentiment gap and asset structure:

$$\widehat{e}_t=>e_t-\overline{e}\propto\pi_e\,|\,\mathbb{o}_t=\log\left(\frac{\Delta\mathcal{E}_{B_D,t}(\mathbb{o}_t)}{\Delta\mathcal{E}_{B_F,t}(\mathbb{o}_t)}\right).$$

This adjustment mechanism diverges sharply from the classic Dornbusch (1976) model, which explains overshooting via sticky prices and interest rate differentials

[6]This would the case when the monetary expansion signals future instability (e.g., fiscal dominance, inflation fears).

under rational expectations. In contrast, SAGE relies on preferences over assets, where the marginal utility of holding foreign versus domestic bonds is directly shaped by evolving sentiment. Rather than assuming nominal rigidities, SAGE explains overshooting as a real-time portfolio rebalancing response to shifts in perceived liquidity and safety, yielding sharper, more persistent exchange rate adjustments even in fully flexible price settings. In this sense, SAGE extends the logic of UIP by embedding it within a utility-theoretic structure, where deviations from UIP reflect not arbitrage inefficiencies but optimal utility reactions under uncertainty and sentiment dynamics.

The adjustment mechanism operates even in the absence of price rigidities or nominal frictions. Depending on circumstances, the monetary shock may fade and expectations slowly revert to their benchmark (as ω_t approaches 1), causing the overshooting to unwind. Alternatively, the shock may not revert for a long time, or it may even worsen, if pessimism feeds on itself. This would create persistent overshooting or even new equilibrium paths: the exchange rate stays weak, portfolio shifts remain unbalanced, and confidence weakens. Conversely, if the monetary authority is highly credible and its policy decision meets with agent optimism, this might even rise longer-term rates and strengthen the exchange rate.

In general, if households infer policy credibility from the central bank's behavior, then sentiment may improve if the expansion is part of a credible strategy (e.g., countercyclical support, not monetization of deficits) or deteriorate if policy is seen as accommodating structural imbalances. Thus, normalization is not automatic, but policy-contingent.

A major advantage of SAGE in this context is its ability to account for *persistent* overshooting without invoking irrational expectations. Instead, equilibrium outcomes depend on utility-based risk premia shaped by sentiment and asset structure. This allows policymakers to distinguish between transient exchange rate misalignments and structurally driven overshooting tied to credibility erosion. Moreover, because sentiment is endogenous and policy-contingent, SAGE offers a tractable framework for evaluating how forward guidance, fiscal-monetary coordination, or credibility-enhancing measures (e.g., inflation targeting, debt rules) can restore exchange rate equilibrium—not by altering arbitrage conditions per se, but by rebalancing utility valuations across assets.

Further extensions could allow for endogenous foreign sentiment formation or interactions with global risk sentiment, e.g., by incorporating foreign investors' utility-based preferences over domestic versus foreign assets. This would open the door to modeling sudden stops, capital flight, and currency crises as equilibrium outcomes of global portfolio reallocations triggered by shifting sentiments (the topic of Sect. 4.6). SAGE thus provides a behavioral-financial microfoundation for understanding extreme exchange rate volatility under rational expectations shaped by evolving sentiment—bridging gaps between behavioral finance, open-economy macroeconomics, and utility theory.

Finally, the exchange rate mechanism envisioned under SAGE represents a concrete extension of the Portfolio Theory of Inflation (PTI),[7] where macroeconomic effectiveness depends on how global investors rebalance portfolios under expectations. This will be the topic of Sect. 4.12.

4.5 Financial Frictions

In its core formulation, SAGE establishes that agents derive utility not only from consumption smoothing or intertemporal substitution, but also from the perceived usability and riskiness of the assets they hold—specifically considering the different "speed" and "power" that assets afford their holders to access real resources, as discussed in Sect. 3.1. Two endogenous factors—liquidation costs ξ_a and price volatility σ_a, for $a \in \{B, K\}$—enter directly into the utility function via an efficiency penalty term. These frictions shape the relative attractiveness of money, bonds, and capital, and form the basis of portfolio allocation. While previous sections model these frictions as asset-specific, this section builds a deeper bridge between financial frictions and financial intermediation, thereby giving institutional structure and propagation power to SAGE's asset-based amplification mechanisms.

Liquidation costs and price volatility are functional outputs of financial market structure and the quality of intermediation. Define:

$$\xi_a = \xi_a(\mathcal{L}_a, I_a) \text{ and } \sigma_a = \sigma_a(\mathcal{D}_a, I_a),$$

where $\mathcal{L}_a$ is the market liquidity of asset a, or the cost and time needed to convert it into consumption; $\mathcal{D}_a$ is the depth of the market for asset a, measuring its price sensitivity to volume shocks; and I_a is the quality of financial intermediation supporting the exchange of asset a (see Sect. 3.1).

Market liquidity and depth are not structural constants: they evolve with sentiment $\mathbb{o}_t$ and institutional quality. Higher intermediation quality I_a improves liquidity and depth, lowering ξ_a and σ_a, and thereby raising the utility efficiency of asset a. This introduces a formal mechanism—a friction differential—by which the financial structure shapes macroeconomic behavior via utility-based choices. Define this friction differential as:

$$\begin{aligned}\Phi_{BK} \mid \mathbb{o}_t, I_{BK} \equiv\ & [\xi_K(\mathcal{L}_K(\mathbb{o}_t), I_K) - \xi_B(\mathcal{L}_B(\mathbb{o}_t), I_B)] \\ & + [\sigma_K(\mathcal{D}_K(\mathbb{o}_t), I_K) - \sigma_B(\mathcal{D}_B(\mathbb{o}_t), I_B)],\end{aligned}$$

with $\frac{\partial \Phi_{BK}}{\partial \mathbb{o}} < 0$ and $\frac{\partial^2 \Phi_{BK}}{\partial \mathbb{o}^2} > 0$. Its curvature gives rise to friction-induced regime shifts whereby, as discussed earlier, even modest shocks can push the economy over a

[7] See Bossone (2025), Chap. 13, "The Portfolio Theory of Inflation and Money (In)Effectiveness," pp. 319–356.

tipping point, beyond which capital becomes effectively non-viable as a utility-bearing asset.

Assets differ not only in return profiles, but in how they are intermediated:

- **Capital** is illiquid, forward-looking, and intermediated through decentralized investment, project finance, equity, and venture markets. I_a includes investor protection, legal frameworks, transparency, and exit options.
- **Government bonds** are intermediated through standardized, centralized, high-volume secondary markets with central clearing. I_a is typically robust and often supported by implicit public guarantees.
- **Money** is frictionless in nominal terms but offers no real return.

As a result, capital typically faces higher baseline ξ_K and σ_K, and is more sensitive to shocks in liquidity and depth—especially when market-making disappears in volatile conditions. In this sense, capital is more vulnerable to amplifying financial frictions, and therefore becomes the primary transmission vector for sentiment shocks in SAGE.

Typically, as pessimistic beliefs take hold, the following chain of events unfolds: agents anticipate increased liquidation pressure and risk premia → market liquidity $\mathcal{L}_K$ and depth $\mathcal{D}_K$ fall → frictions ξ_K and σ_K rise nonlinearly, especially when I_K is weak → friction differential Φ_{BK} rises → optimal portfolio allocations shifts from capital to bonds → investment and innovation collapse, reinforcing pessimism.

To see how this sequence may evolve differently in contexts with different financial systems, consider two economies, 1 and 2, with hypothetically identical fundamentals but different capital intermediation quality: economy 1 has a mature equity market, strong legal protections, and deep liquidity, while economy 2 has fragmented investment channels, weak enforcement, and opaque governance.

Under a global shock, both economies face falling sentiment. However:

- In economy 1, ξ_K and σ_K rise only modestly;
- In economy 2, shallow liquidity and fragile depth amplify friction shocks;
- Φ_{BK} increases steeply in economy 2, triggering flight from capital and collapse of investment.

SAGE predicts divergent macro outcomes based not on policy rates or fiscal space, but on intermediation resilience—a channel often overlooked in standard macro theory. Without entering the policy dimension, which is outside the scope of this book, it can be noted that this reconceptualization of financial frictions as institutional and utility penalties renders SAGE highly actionable, as it calls for targeted interventions—such as strengthening intermediation infrastructure, deploying market-maker-of-last-resort operations, adopting friction-sensitive macroprudential tools, enhancing legal credibility, and activating state-contingent public intermediation—that act not on credit supply per se but on the utility efficiency of asset markets, where expectations and real behavior converge.

To conclude, by embedding liquidation costs and price volatility within the structure of market liquidity and depth, mediated by intermediation quality, SAGE bridges microeconomic choice and price theory, institutional finance, and macroeconomic outcomes. In doing so, it explains how expectations propagate through friction dynamics and why economies with similar fundamentals diverge sharply under stress. SAGE thereby offers a structurally grounded and empirically rich framework to study not only macroeconomic instability, but also the institutional prerequisites of resilience.

It should be noted, finally, that while SAGE is here built on a minimalistic role of the financial sector, for the purpose of giving greater emphasis to household portfolio choices (see Sect. 3.2), the utility-based framework underpinning SAGE can be used to model the proper role of financial intermediation, including at the global level.[8]

4.6 Sudden Stops and Capital Flow Reversals

Sudden stops and sharp reversals in net capital flows are among the most destabilizing macro-financial phenomena faced by financially open economies. Characterized by abrupt foreign investor retrenchment, collapsing asset prices, exchange rate depreciation, and output contraction, sudden stops can occur with little change in fundamentals and often exhibit persistence far beyond the initial trigger. Traditional models tend to rely on ad hoc mechanisms such as exogenous shocks, sunspot equilibria, or balance sheet constraints to explain them (Calvo, 1998; Mendoza, 2002). In contrast, SAGE explains sudden stops and capital flow reversals as endogenous portfolio reallocations driven by sentiment-contingent expectations of rational global investors acting in response to perceived changes in asset efficiency, institutional trust, and macroeconomic stability.

Let a representative global investor allocate wealth $\mathcal{W}_t$ across a vector of assets $a \in A$, where $A \in \{a_H, a_F\}$ and a_H and a_F refer, respectively, to assets from a domestic economy H (home) and the rest of the world F (foreign). The investor maximizes utility over real consumption-equivalent holdings, adjusted by efficiency discount factors that reflect asset transaction frictions and price volatility. At each date t, the investor solves:

$$\max_{=\{a_H, a_F\}} \theta_H(\mathbb{O}_t)\, log\left(\frac{P_{H,t}a_{H,t}}{P_{C,t}\left[1+\xi_{H,t}(\mathbb{O}_t)+\sigma_{H,t}(\mathbb{O}_t)\right]}\right)$$

$$+\,\theta_F(\mathbb{O}_t)\, log\left(\frac{P_{F,t}a_{F,t}}{P_{C,t}\left[1+\xi_{F,t}(\mathbb{O}_t)+\sigma_{F,t}(\mathbb{O}_t)\right]}\right)$$

subject to:

[8] See Bossone (2025), Chap. 13, cit.

$$P_{H,t}a_{H,t} + P_{F,t}a_{F,t} = W_t$$

The home asset utility is increasing in sentiment $\frac{\partial u_t(a_H)}{\partial \text{\textcircled{o}}_t} > 0$ and its gross efficiency discount factor improves with sentiment $\frac{\partial \Delta \mathcal{E} a_{H,t}}{\partial \text{\textcircled{o}}_t} < 0$.[9]

A **sudden stop** emerges as $\text{\textcircled{o}}_t \to 0$, whereby sentiment-induced deterioration in perceived liquidity and price volatility raises $\mathcal{E}_{a_H}$ and depresses $u_t(a_H)$. When

$$u_t(a_H) < u_t(a_F) \Rightarrow \frac{\partial \Delta \mathcal{E}^*_{a_H,t}}{\partial \text{\textcircled{o}}_t} < 0,$$

the optimal portfolio reallocation away from domestic assets accelerates. This captures the empirical observation that capital flow reversals are nonlinear and often disproportionately large relative to observable fundamentals. The convexity of $\Delta \mathcal{E}_{a_H,t}(\text{\textcircled{o}}_t)$ implies that small further declines in already-low sentiment lead to large utility losses and sudden capital exits.

As discussed in Sects. 3.1 and 4.6, within SAGE, the efficiency discount factors $\Delta \mathcal{E}_a{}'s$ are shaped not only by sentiment but also by the S&E of the institutional and financial infrastructure supporting asset liquidation and price volatility—formally $\xi_a = \xi_a(\psi, \text{\textcircled{o}}_t)$ and $\sigma_a = \sigma_a(\psi, \text{\textcircled{o}}_t)$. Any deterioration in institutional quality—such as loss of central bank independence, fiscal dominance, sovereign default risk, or erratic policymaking—lowers ψ, lengthens the optimal asset sale time $\Delta \tau^*_q$, and thereby raises asset liquidation costs ξ_a and price volatilty σ_a, reinforcing the collapse in $u_t(a)$. This mechanism structurally explains why sudden stops are more likely in jurisdictions with weak or deteriorating institutions, even absent immediate macroeconomic distress.

Empirical literature supports this transmission channel. Calvo et al. (2004) show that institutional indicators strongly predict the onset of sudden stops. Broner et al. (2013) demonstrate that countries with weak credibility and financial institutions experience more volatile capital flows and sharper reversals.

Once capital begins to exit, the resulting price volatility further raises $\sigma_{H,\,t}$, while fire-sale dynamics and shortening liquidation windows further raise $\xi_{H,\,t}$. The gross efficiency discount factor $\Delta \mathcal{E}_{a_H,t}(\text{\textcircled{o}}_t)$ thus rises endogenously, feeding back into lower a_H utility. This recursive feedback loop mirrors boom–bust cycles and secular stagnation traps discussed in Sects. 4.1 and 4.2, now applied to the external sector. In the limit, if sentiment remains deeply pessimistic, the system converges to an **external stagnation trap**:

$$\lim_{\text{\textcircled{o}}_t \to 0} \Rightarrow \lim_{t \to \infty} a^*_{H,t} = 0,$$

[9] Recall that the efficiency discount factor of any asset a is the inverse of $\partial \Delta \mathcal{E} a_{,t}$.Thus, as sentiment improves, the effect of the discount diminishes, and vice versa.

that is, global investors asymptotically abandon domestic assets, regardless of their intrinsic returns, and exit the domestic markets so that it becomes an optimal choice for investors to get rid of asset a_H altogether. This reflects not irrational panic, but endogenous dislocation due to rising utility discounts on domestic assets. The economy enters a persistent disinvestment trap that can be reversed only by rebuilding sentiment and institutional credibility. Recovery from such a trap requires not just improved fundamentals but coordinated changes that boost sentiment $\mathbb{O}_t$ and lower the gross efficiency discount factor $\Delta\mathcal{E}_{a_H,t}$, particularly via institutional and policy credibility improvements.

SAGE also endogenizes currency depreciation as a rational adjustment to collapsing money utility. As sentiment toward the domestic economy falls, the utility of holding money domestic currency M_H declines since $\frac{\partial u_t(M_H)}{\partial \mathbb{O}_t} > 0$, due to the circumstance that money's gross efficiency discount factor $\Delta\mathcal{E}_{M_H,t}(\mathbb{O}_t)$ increases. This causes the demand for M_H to fall and its exchange rate to depreciate vis-à-vis stronger currencies. This logic parallels Sect. 4.4, where depreciation results from shifts in portfolio preferences.

In managed exchange rate regimes, the central bank may intervene with foreign exchange reserves or interest rate hikes. However, unless such actions credibly restore expectations and reduce money's gross efficiency discount factor $\Delta\mathcal{E}_{M_H,t}$, they may fail to reverse capital outflows. Monetary tools are effective only if they address the underlying sentiment and improve the perceived safety and liquidity of domestic assets.

Episodes such as Argentina in 2018–2019) and Turkey in 2021 illustrate SAGE-consistent sudden stop dynamics. In both cases, capital outflows were triggered by rising political uncertainty, loss of policy credibility, and legal or institutional concerns. These dynamics coincided with falling $\mathbb{O}_t$, rising $\Delta\mathcal{E}_{a_H,t}$, and depreciating exchange rates—even in the absence of immediate solvency concerns. This supports SAGE view of sudden stops as endogenous, sentiment-influenced revaluations of utility-based asset quality.

In conclusion, SAGE reframes sudden stops not as market failures or exogenous crises, but as equilibrium outcomes of sentiment-influenced rational reallocations of global portfolios under utility. It offers both a conceptual advance in macro-financial modeling and a foundation for designing resilience-enhancing institutions and credibility-sensitive policy responses.

4.7 Global Portfolio Asymmetries

One of the most persistent and theoretically unsettling facts in international economics is the asymmetry of global capital flows: capital tends not to flow from rich to poor countries—even when the marginal productivity of capital (MPK) is substantially higher in the latter. This observation, first formalized as the **Lucas Paradox** (Lucas, 1990), defies the predictions of neoclassical models, which suggest that financial capital should flow "downhill" to where it earns the highest real return. Compounding this paradox is the phenomenon of **global savings gluts** and persistent current account imbalances, whereby developing and emerging economies accumulate foreign reserves and export capital to advanced economies—despite lower income levels and vast domestic investment needs (Bernanke, 2005; Gourinchas & Rey, 2014).

The Lucas Paradox

Assume global investors allocate wealth between home and foreign assets as in Sect. 4.6, and consider a representative poor country with a high MPK but low institutional quality. In a neoclassical world, capital should flow toward that country, attracted by high returns. On the other hand, in SAGE world, investors optimize not over expected MPK alone, but over utility-based returns, incorporating transaction frictions, price volatility, and sentiment.

Take country H with weak legal enforcement, volatile macro policies, or unpredictable political risk. It will be perceived as inefficient even if its MPK is high. This emerges from considering that the effective utility of high-return asset K in country H, K_H, to global investors holding it is given by:

$$u_t(K_H) = \theta_{K_H}(\mathfrak{o}_t)\, log\left(\frac{MPK_H}{\Delta\mathcal{E}_{K_H,t}(\mathfrak{o}_t)}\right), \tag{4.3}$$

where MPK represents the theoretical benchmark for capital allocation efficiency in a neoclassical world. Clearly as $\Delta\mathcal{E}_{a_H,t}(\mathfrak{o}_t) \gg 1$, this would offset the high MPK in Eq. (4.3) and $u_t(a_H)$ would be heavily discounted as a result. The paradox is resolved: capital does not flow to high-MPK destinations, because the utility of doing so is too low once frictions are accounted for. Ju and Wei (2010) show that weak domestic institutions lead to "bypass" behavior in financial globalization—global capital avoids the domestic sector even when it offers higher raw returns. This effect is structurally embedded in SAGE's sentiment-adjusted frictions.

This mechanism was clearly visible in China during the 2000s, where, despite a high *MPK* and a strong growth trajectory, the country experienced massive capital outflows and accumulated foreign exchange reserves exceeding USD 3 trillion. These patterns reflected low global and domestic $\mathfrak{o}_t$: global investors distrusted Chinese capital markets, while Chinese savers and institutions preferred offshore assets or dollar reserves due to underdeveloped local financial intermediation, weak legal protections, and political risk. SAGE captures this behavior as a rational portfolio response to a sentiment-contingent discount on domestic capital allocation, despite favorable economic fundamentals.

It is important to emphasize that SAGE does not reject MPK as a driver of capital flows; rather, it reframes MPK as one element within a broader sentiment-contingent utility function. Potential returns alone are insufficient if they are deeply discounted by high perceived frictions or low institutional credibility. In this sense, capital misallocation arises not from irrationality or market failure, but from endogenous beliefs about risk and efficiency.

The Savings Glut and Reserves Accumulation

SAGE also offers a structural interpretation of the global savings glut as a rational excess demand for safe, high-utility assets. Emerging markets, particularly after the 1997 Asian financial crisis, began accumulating reserves and investing in advanced-economy sovereign bonds—not because of a lack of investment needs, but because:

- Their own financial systems were perceived as unsafe or inefficient (low ϖ_t, high $\Delta\mathcal{E}_{a_H,t}$);
- Domestic political or institutional instability reduced the perceived utility of local investment; and
- The global risk sentiment shifted toward capital preservation, amplifying the preference for liquid, trusted assets (U.S. Treasuries, German Bunds, etc.).

Letting the representative sovereign or institutional investor in a surplus country solve:

$$\max_{a_t} \theta_a(\varpi_t)\, log\left(\frac{P^*_{a,t}a_t}{P_{C,t}\Delta\mathcal{E}_{a,t}(\varpi_t)}\right),$$

where $a_t \in \{a_F, K_H\}$, a_F is low-risk foreign reserves, and K_H is high-risk domestic capital, and where $\Delta\mathcal{E}_{a_F,t}(\varpi_t) < \Delta\mathcal{E}_{K_H,t}(\varpi_t)$, $\frac{\partial\Delta\mathcal{E}_{a_F,t}(\varpi_t)}{\partial\varpi_t} < 0$, and $\frac{\partial\Delta\mathcal{E}_{K_H,t}(\varpi_t)}{\partial\varpi_t} > 0$. Under these assumptions, whereas sentiment deterioration increases the efficiency discount of domestic capital, making it less attractive, the same decreases the efficiency discount of foreign reserves, making it more attractive as a safe-haven asset for the investors. As a result, under condition of high perceived risk and uncertainty, even capital-rich countries prefer holding low-yield foreign assets, leading to sustained global imbalances, whereby national saving exceeds investment in surplus countries not because MPK is low but because expectations are pessimistic, and vice versa in deficit countries: capital does not flow where returns are highest. It flows where assets are most trusted.

This mechanism also plays out at the level of domestic households and institutions. Under low ϖ_t, even local agents prefer to allocate wealth offshore, either directly (via capital flight) or indirectly (via bank deposits that are converted into foreign reserves by the central bank). SAGE thus endogenizes not only global investor behavior, but also domestic precautionary saving and capital allocation.

A compelling example of SAGE's explanatory power is India's post-2013 transition. Following major reforms in monetary and fiscal governance, coupled with improvements in financial infrastructure and institutional transparency, global investor sentiment toward India improved markedly. This was reflected in rising capital inflows, narrowing risk premia, and declining precautionary reserve accumulation—even though the underlying MPK changed only gradually. The shift was not in fundamentals per se, but in the sentiment-adjusted perception of efficiency and safety. SAGE anticipates exactly this kind of credibility-induced reallocation dynamic.

SAGE implies that sentiment asymmetries across countries are central to the global capital structure. Countries with high ω_t are perceived as safe havens, regardless of their fundamental returns, while those with low ω_t face persistent underallocation of global capital. And when global sentiment turns sour, countries perceived as more credible attract more capital from all others. Notice that SAGE does not require a high ω_t overall, but a gap in sentiment between asset classes. This has several important consequences:

- **Reserves concentration**: Demand for advanced-economy safe assets outstrips supply, depressing yields and reinforcing low investment incentives globally;
- **Trapped capital**: Developing countries cannot access sufficient financing to exploit their growth potential, contributing to slow convergence;
- **Global liquidity asymmetry**: High- ω_t countries provide liquidity, while low-ω_t countries hoard reserves for self-insurance;
- **Policy ineffectiveness**: Structural reforms may raise MPK, but unless they also improve perceived efficiency and sentiment, capital inflows may remain subdued.

SAGE's explanation for global portfolio asymmetries is consistent with the empirical literature. Alfaro et al. (2008) show that institutional quality is a stronger determinant of foreign direct investment than MPK. Gourinchas and Jeanne (2013) document that investment efficiency, not capital scarcity, explains cross-country differences in capital inflows. Caballero et al. (2008) identify a global shortage of safe assets, driven by a mismatch between investor preferences and perceived asset quality. These findings validate SAGE's core claim: capital flows are utility-optimized allocations, not mechanical responses to MPK or interest differentials.

4.8 The Drivers of Growth

In conventional growth theory, long-run economic growth is typically modeled as a consequence of the accumulation of capital and human capital and the exogenous or innovation-driven evolution of total factor productivity (TFP). Preferences, expectations, and frictions are often treated as stable or exogenous features of the environment. This abstraction fails to explain real-world asymmetries such as underinvestment in high-MPK economies, persistent labor detachment, or sudden growth reversals despite stable fundamentals.

SAGE offers a different perspective. It treats growth as a product of intra- and inter-temporal optimization under uncertainty, shaped by the interaction between reason (structured knowledge and rational foresight) and sentiment (emotional orientation and social mood). Agents allocate consumption, labor, capital, and education effort by continuously updating their expectations through the rational use of knowledge, the processing of the information available, and prevailing sentiment ω_t.

Growth is not just about capital deepening or technological progress—it is about whether agents believe that intertemporal investments will pay off, under institutional conditions they trust, with risk-adjusted returns that reflect more than just fundamentals.

The foundation of SAGE is the recursive optimization problem faced by a representative agent:

$$V(s_t) = \max_{x_t} \{U(C_t, M_t, B_t, K_t, \mathcal{K}_t, L_t; \mathbb{O}_t) + \beta \mathbb{E}_t[V(s_{t+1})\}, \tag{4.4}$$

where $s_t = \{K_t, \mathcal{K}_t, L_t, \mathbb{O}_t, \xi_t, \sigma_t, A_t\}$ denote the vector of state variables, with $\mathcal{K}$ representing human capital, and $x_t = \{C_t, a_{K,t}, a_{\mathcal{K},t}, L_t\}$ are the control variables. The agent's first-order conditions determine optimal effort allocations. Taking the Euler equation for capital obtains:

$$\frac{\partial U_t}{\partial C_t} = \beta \mathbb{E}_t \left[\frac{\partial V_{t+1}}{\partial K_{t+1}} r^e_{K,t+1} \right] = \beta \mathbb{E}_t \left[\frac{\partial V_{t+1}}{\partial \mathcal{K}_{t+1}} r^e_{\mathcal{K},t+1} \right]$$

where

$$r^e_{K,t+1} = \frac{\mathbb{E}_t[r_{K,t+1}]}{\Delta\mathcal{E}_{K,t}(\mathbb{O}_t)} = \frac{\mathbb{E}_t[r_{\mathcal{K},t+1}]}{\Delta\mathcal{E}_{\mathcal{K},t}(\mathbb{O}_t)} = r^e_{\mathcal{K},t+1}$$

are the effective expected rates of return on productive (tangible or intangible) capital and human capital, respectively, that is, the returns reduced by their respective effective sentiment-contingent gross discount factors $\Delta\mathcal{E}_{K,t}(\mathbb{O}_t)$ and $\Delta\mathcal{E}_{\mathcal{K},t}(\mathbb{O}_t)$, which reflect the agents' effective incentive to invest in the two types of capital.

Solving Eq. (4.4) for each of the control variables determines the optimal micro-level intra- and inter-temporal allocation choices. These allocations are then inserted in production function:

$$Y_t = Y\left(\frac{K_t}{\Delta\mathcal{E}_{K,t}(\mathbb{O}_t)}, \frac{\mathcal{K}_t}{\Delta\mathcal{E}_{\mathcal{K},t}(\mathbb{O}_t)}, \frac{L_t}{\Delta\mathcal{E}_{L,t}(\mathbb{O}_t)}, A_t \right), \tag{4.5}$$

where the variables in K, $\mathcal{K}$, and L denote the effective inputs, i.e., the portion of the raw inputs that actually contributes to output, after accounting for distortions originating from frictions,[10] and where

$$A_t = A(\mathbb{O}_t, \psi_t) \tag{4.6}$$

[10]Frictions here refer to any obstacle or inefficiency that prevents an input from being fully utilized or from delivering its maximum potential return. These include financial frictions (e.g., high liquidation costs, liquidity constraints, or credit rationing), institutional frictions e.g., (weak legal protections, policy uncertainty, or lack of trust, and sentiment-driven distortions (e.g., fear, uncertainty, pessimism).

is TFP, with $\frac{\partial A}{\partial \mathrm{o}}, \frac{\partial A}{\partial \psi} > 0$, that is, TFP grows with agent confidence and with the level of S&E of the financial system. This explains why declining sentiment or institutional deterioration can result in declining TFP—even without negative shocks to technology itself. Aggregate output growth is then given by:

$$g_t = \frac{Y_t - Y_{t-1}}{Y_{t-1}} = g\left(\varrho_{K,t}, \varrho_{\mathcal{K},t}; \mathrm{o}_t, \psi_t\right) \tag{4.7}$$

where

$$\varrho_{K,t} = \frac{K_t}{\Delta\mathcal{E}_{K,t}(\mathrm{o}_t)} \frac{1}{\mathcal{W}} \text{ and } \varrho_{\mathcal{K},t} = \frac{\mathcal{K}_t}{\Delta\mathcal{E}_{\mathcal{K},t}(\mathrm{o}_t)} \frac{1}{\mathcal{W}} \tag{4.8}$$

are, respectively, the share of the agent's wealth or portfolio allocated to effective productive capital and human capital at time t, conditional on sentiment and financial system S&E. These shares capture how much capital accumulation occurs as a share of the total asset allocation, given prevailing sentiment and financial frictions.

Notice that, in equilibrium, the share of capital in wealth must reflect the expected effective return on capital. Thus:

$$\varrho^*_{K,t} = \frac{K^*_t}{\Delta\mathcal{E}_{K,t}(\mathrm{o}_t)} \frac{1}{\mathcal{W}} = \frac{\mathbb{E}_t\left[r^*_{,t+1}\right]}{\Delta\mathcal{E}_{\mathcal{K},t}(\mathrm{o}_t)} = r^{e^*}_{\mathcal{K},t+1}. \tag{4.9}$$

Notice also that $\varrho_{K,\ t}$ and $\varrho_{\mathcal{K},t}$ reflect the *endogenous response* of capital to sentiment and (broadly speaking) institutional conditions. Based on Eqs. (4.4)–(4.9), growth emerges as the result of portfolio choices, determined by the recursive optimization problem.

Importantly, these equations reveal that long-run growth in SAGE is driven not by the aggregate level of saving, but by its allocation across assets. Effective capital shares $\varrho_{K,\ t}$ and $\varrho_{\mathcal{K},t}$, which determine output growth g_t, are functions of both expected returns and sentiment-contingent discount factors $\Delta\mathcal{E}_{K,t}(\mathrm{o}_t)$ and $\Delta\mathcal{E}_{\mathcal{K},t}(\mathrm{o}_t)$. These discount factors capture how sentiment distorts intertemporal valuations, thereby altering the relative attractiveness of illiquid, long-horizon investments versus liquid or defensive assets. Even when objective fundamentals favor productive and human capital accumulation, a pessimistic or volatile sentiment regime can raise $\Delta\mathcal{E}_{K,t}$ and $\Delta\mathcal{E}_{\mathcal{K},t}$, suppressing effective returns $r_{K,\ t+1}$ and $r_{\mathcal{K},t+1}$ and reducing capital allocation. Since the production function depends on effective inputs rather than raw quantities, and since these effective inputs are endogenously shaped by portfolio choices, growth becomes a consequence of how saving is composed—not how much is saved.

Sentiment and Growth Regimes

In SAGE, growth is contingent on sentiment as encoded by the indicator $\mathrm{o}_t = \frac{\Omega'_t}{\Omega_t} \in (0, \infty), \Omega_t, \Omega'_t \in (0, 1)$, introduced in Sect. 3.1, where Ω_t reflects the state of information and knowledge available to agents and precision, and Ω_t' reflects the agents' emotional orientation. This indicator determines whether agents are sentimentally biased in optimistic ($\omega_t > 1$) or pessimistic ($\omega_t < 1$) directions, and thereby affects how they interpret returns, risks, and constraints.

As discussed, different combinations of these dimensions define distinct sentiment regimes, each associated with characteristic macroeconomic behaviors. The four archetypal regions into which these behaviors can be categorized are the following:

1. **Rational pessimism** $\left(\Omega_t \approx 1, \Omega_t' \ll 1 \Rightarrow \omega_t \ll 1\right)$. Characterized by high saving, low investment, falling TFP, disinflation, secular stagnation. In this region, agents hold accurate but bleak expectations—reflecting a deep recognition of adverse fundamentals. Investment and effort collapse despite good information. An example of this regime is Japan's post-1990 economy.
2. **Speculative optimism** $\left(\Omega_t \ll 1, \Omega_t' \gg 1 \Rightarrow \omega_t \gg 1\right)$. Characterized by high leverage, asset booms, rising inequality, vulnerability to busts. Here agents' confidence exceeds informational grounding. Overinvestment and misallocation dominate, producing asset bubbles. Examples of this growth regime are the U.S. tech boom of 1995–2000 and pre-2008 credit expansion.
3. **Rational optimism** $\left(\Omega_t \approx \Omega_t' \gg 1 \Rightarrow \omega_t \approx 1\right)$. Characterized by steady growth, high $\alpha_{k,t}$, $\alpha_{k,t}$, efficient capital-labor balance. Here, a balance of confidence and informational rigor supports stable, productive growth. This regime approximates ideal conditions for SAGE-efficient capital allocation. The steady growth of Germany during 2006–2016 is an example of this growth regime.
4. **Volatile Indeterminacy** $\left(\Omega_t, \Omega_t' \ll 1 \Rightarrow \omega_t \approx 1\right)$. Characterized by policy ineffectiveness, cyclical instability, swings in capital flows. Here, agents lack both reliable information and clear orientation. Behavior becomes erratic, sensitive to noise or fads. Growth outcomes are volatile and coordination failures frequent. The experience of various emerging economies in various epochs recalls this type of growth regime.

The Advantages of SAGE

SAGE growth theory introduces a novel paradigm by structurally integrating sentiment into the foundational mechanics of long-run growth. Building on the recursive optimization structure and production function developed in this section, SAGE offers a unified explanation for why economies grow, stagnate, or collapse—even under identical fundamentals—by placing human sentiment and rational intra- and inter-temporal choices at the center of analysis. Its advantages vis-à-vis conventional growth theories are the following:

First, SAGE endogenizes behaviorally coherent growth dynamics. It breaks from neoclassical and endogenous growth models that rely on stable preferences, fixed innovation schedules, or exogenous shocks. Through sentiment indicator ω_t, the model makes portfolio decisions (capital allocation, labor effort, human capital investment) contingent on how agents emotionally interpret reality. This renders boom–bust dynamics, stagnation traps, and growth hysteresis as emergent outcomes of optimal behavior, not anomalies.

Second, SAGE provides microfoundations for growth reversals and underperformance. Phenomena such as the Lucas paradox (see Sect. 4.6)—the failure of capital to flow to high-MPK regions—or post-crisis productivity collapse are often unexplained by conventional theory. In SAGE, these phenomena result from endogenous rises in inefficiency and drops in perceived return precision when sentiment declines. Even when objective fundamentals suggest high returns, agents with low sentiment experience diminished expected utility, diverting resources away from productive uses.

Third, SAGE redefines the role of total factor productivity. TFP is not residual or driven purely by technological exogeneity; it is modeled as a function $A_t = A(\varpi_t, \psi_t)$, shaped by sentiment and institutional factors (see Eq. (4.6)). This formulation allows SAGE to explain episodes where reforms or innovations fail to yield growth due to insufficient trust or optimism, aligning better with empirical cases of delayed takeoff or reform fatigue.

Fourth, SAGE models sentiment-contingent transitions across multiple growth regimes. As formalized in the above typology, combinations of informational precision and orientation generate divergent ϖ_t values, resulting in distinct equilibria—rational optimism, rational pessimism, speculative exuberance, or indeterminate paralysis. These help explain why some economies rebound while others stall, even under similar policy inputs or shocks.

Fifth, SAGE generalizes and unifies the insights of endogenous growth, behavioral macroeconomics, and neoclassical portfolio theory. It accommodates innovation, education, and institutional quality, while also capturing feedback loops between beliefs, actions, and outcomes. By embedding growth drivers within a sentiment-aware recursive structure, SAGE yields internally coherent and empirically plausible predictions without invoking exogenous shocks or artificial parameter shifts (see Sect. 4.9). In a broader understanding, sentiment will then be analyzed as a deep structural driver that shapes the effectiveness and allocation of growth inputs over time (Sect. 4.10).

Sixth and final, and very importantly, in SAGE, long-run growth is not determined by aggregate saving per se, but by the composition of saving across different assets. What matters is not how much agents defer consumption, but how they allocate intertemporal resources—whether into liquid stores of value or into illiquid, longer-horizon productive assets. Growth accelerates when sentiment supports patient allocation toward illiquid but high-utility investments, and when institutions, technologies, and narratives reduce the transaction costs and price volatility associated with such assets. Conversely, even high aggregate saving may fail to support growth if fear, mistrust, or fragility drive agents toward defensive, liquid, or speculative allocations. SAGE thus redefines the growth question in portfolio terms: not how much is saved for the future, but what kind of future is being funded by the composition of savings.

4.9 Endogenous Growth Under Liquidity and Portfolio Constraints

In this section, the SAGE framework is used to examine how growth emerges endogenously from households' intra- and inter-temporal utility maximization and firms' innovation behavior under financial frictions. For reasons of simplicity, but without loss of generality, human capital is not treated separately in the following analysis and, instead, it is embedded in productive capital.

This section develops a model of TFP growth that endogenizes the transformation of capital into innovation, subject to asset liquidation costs and asset price volatility. The key insight is that the growth process is mediated by portfolio allocation decisions: the willingness of agents to hold long-duration, high-volatility capital assets shapes the availability and effectiveness of innovation finance. As we show, innovation intensity and productivity growth are not simply functions of technology and resources, but depend critically on the dynamic interaction between perceived liquidity, volatility, and utility across time.

As seen, in SAGE, long-run growth emerges from rational portfolio decisions made under preferences for liquidity, risk, and returns in an uncertain world. SAGE endogenizes productivity growth—the backbone of long-term economic growth—as a function of capital allocation decisions driven by rational expectations shaped by sentiment.

Take Eq. (3.13) above,

$$A_{t+1} = A_t(1 + \phi_I I_t), \text{with } I_t = k \frac{K_t}{\Delta\mathcal{E}_{K,t}(\mathbb{o}_t)}.$$

The gross efficiency discount factor $\Delta\mathcal{E}_{K,t} = 1 + \xi_{K_t}(\mathbb{o}_t) + \sigma_{K_t}(\mathbb{o}_t)$ increases with the liquidation cost ξ_{K_t} and price volatility σ_{K_t}, shaped by the prevailing sentiment $\mathbb{o}_t$. This formulation captures the notion that even when physical capital K_t is available, innovation capital is reduced if risk-adjusted frictions increase. Taking logs and differentiating Eq. (3.13), the endogenous rate of productivity growth is:

$$g_{A,t} := \log\left(\frac{A_{t+1}}{A_t}\right) \approx k \frac{K_t}{\Delta\mathcal{E}_{K,t}(\mathbb{o}_t)}.$$

This highlights that productivity growth depends jointly on capital holdings and sentiment-conditioned efficiency losses. The nonlinearity in this function underpins the emergence of multiple growth regimes.

To understand growth potential, define the sentiment-conditioned growth potential function

$$K(\text{o}_t) := \frac{K_t}{\Delta\varepsilon_{K,t}(\text{o}_t)} \tag{4.10}$$

to express the effective capital available for innovation, net of frictions—that is, how much usable capital is directed toward productivity-enhancing innovation once sentiment orientations are factored in. Define also:

$$K(\text{o}^C) = \frac{\theta_K}{\lambda_t P_{K_t} \Delta\varepsilon^2_{K,t}(\text{o}^C)} \equiv K^C$$

as the minimum threshold level of effective capital needed to generate positive self-sustaining productivity growth. Finally, define two growth regimes based on $\kappa(\text{o}_t)$ relative to the critical threshold:

- Growth regime $\mathbb{G}^C$: $K(\text{o}_t) \geq K^C \Longrightarrow g_{A,t} \geq g^C > 0$.
- Growth regime $\mathbb{G}^S$: $K(\text{o}_t) < K^C \Longrightarrow g_{A,t} \approx 0$.

This formalization makes $K(\text{o}_t)$ the central determinant of long-run growth. Since $\varepsilon_{K,t}(\text{o}_t)$ encapsulates inefficiencies, solving Eq. (4.10) for o_t yields the sentiment threshold o^c at which the growth dynamic bifurcates:

$$\Delta\varepsilon_{K,t}(\text{o}_t) < \Delta\varepsilon_{K,t}(\text{o}^C) = \sqrt{\frac{\theta_K \lambda_t}{K^*}} \Longrightarrow \text{o}_t \geq \text{o}^C \tag{4.11}$$

and conversely:

$$\Delta\varepsilon_{K,t}(\text{o}_t) \geq \Delta\varepsilon_{K,t}(\text{o}^C) = \sqrt{\frac{\theta_K \lambda_t}{K^*}} \Longrightarrow \text{o}_t < \text{o}^C \text{ (stagnation regime)}. \tag{4.12}$$

The threshold, thus, demarcates a critical tipping point: when sentiment stays above or equals o^C, growth is self-sustainable, Eq. (4.11); when sentiment drops below o^C, the sentiment-contingent capital level drops below the required level to sustain growth, Eq. (4.12). The derivative of innovation with respect to sentiment is:

$$\frac{\partial I_t}{\partial \text{o}_t} = \eta_K \left(\frac{\partial K_t}{\partial \text{o}_t} \frac{1}{\Delta\varepsilon_{K,t}} - \frac{\partial K_t}{\partial \text{o}_t} \frac{1}{\Delta\varepsilon^2_{K,t}} \right). \tag{4.13}$$

Given that capital demand increases with sentiment, $\frac{\partial K_t}{\partial \text{o}_t} > 0$, and the capital efficiency discount factor declines with sentiment, $\frac{\partial \Delta\varepsilon_{K,t}}{\partial \text{o}_t} < 0$, the derivative in Eq. (4.13) is strictly positive and convex. This implies that even marginal increases in optimism near o^C (from above) can induce a nonlinear acceleration in innovation effort, pushing the system into sustained growth. This dynamic is further reinforced by the capital return feedback:

$$r_{K,t} = \frac{\alpha A_t \left(\frac{K_t}{L_t}\right)^{a-1}}{P_{K,t}} \Rightarrow \frac{\partial r_{K,t}}{\partial \mathbb{o}_t} = \frac{\partial r_{K,t}}{\partial A_t} \frac{\partial A_t}{\partial \mathbb{o}_t} > 0.$$

As productivity and capital rise under optimistic beliefs (which lower $\Delta\mathcal{E}_{K,t}$), capital returns increase, reinforcing incentives to hold capital and further improving innovation efficiency.

Notice that because of the curvature of $\Delta\mathcal{E}_{K,t}(\mathbb{o}_t)$ and the feedback between sentiment and innovation, the system exhibits path dependence. Assuming, as before, that sentiment evolves according to $\mathbb{o}_t = Prob(\mathbb{o}_{t-1}, \varepsilon_t)$ where ε_t is a noise term, then, if $\mathbb{o}_t \geq \mathbb{o}^C$, the system remains in a state with stable productivity growth. Such growth would remain positive, though weakening, even if $\mathbb{o}_{t-1} > \mathbb{o}_t \geq \mathbb{o}^C$.

If, on the other hand, a shock pushes sentiment considerably down, such that $\mathbb{o}_t < \mathbb{o}^C$, a transition to the stagnation regime $\mathbb{O}^S$ could occur and turn out to be absorbing: $Prob(\mathbb{o}_{t+1} \geq \mathbb{o}^C | \mathbb{o}_t < \mathbb{o}^C) \ll 1$. This would introduce sentiment-contingent hysteresis: the economy can get trapped in a stagnation path (analyzed in the previous chapter) even if fundamentals are unchanged. Unlike in traditional endogenous growth models, the economy's growth path is non-ergodic and is shaped by the trajectory of expectations.

Episodes such as Italy's post-2008 economic malaise or Eurozone stagnation following the 2011 debt crisis may be illustrative of economies trapped below the sentiment threshold $\mathbb{o}^C$, where capital inefficiencies prevent self-sustaining growth despite ample saving resources. Conversely, the U.S. recovery from the Great Depression or China's boom since joining the WTO exemplify sharp transitions into growth-supportive regimes, driven by credible policy and sentiment restoration. These country economies should be examined as real-world cases providing validation to the bifurcation logic of SAGE.

SAGE endogenous growth model builds upon, and generalizes, traditional endogenous growth theory by embedding capital accumulation and innovation into a portfolio allocation framework. In standard models such as Romer (1990) or Aghion and Howitt (1992), long-run growth arises from innovation or knowledge spillovers fueled by investment in research or human capital. These models assume agents optimize inter-temporally under stable preferences and rational expectations. In contrast, SAGE endogenizes the effectiveness of innovation-related investment by making it conditional on agents' beliefs about liquidity, risk, and return under uncertainty—captured through the capital efficiency factor $\Delta\mathcal{E}_{K,t}(\mathbb{o}_t)$. This allows the model to account for time-varying innovation efficiency and sentiment-induced frictions that amplify or suppress the productivity of capital.

While SAGE retains the neoclassical insight that capital accumulation drives long-term growth, it introduces a behavioral-financial channel through which rational expectations shaped by sentiments dynamically alter the marginal efficiency of capital, thus endogenizing growth regimes and their stability properties. In this sense, SAGE integrates the structural core of endogenous growth theory within a more general, utility-theoretic framework.

4.10 Sentiment and Long-Run Growth

While the previous section has formalized the endogenous growth mechanism within the SAGE framework—highlighting the central role of capital allocation, innovation shares, and financial frictions—this section broadens the analytical lens. It interprets long-run growth not only as a function of economic optimization, but as the outcome of a deeper sentiment regime that shapes expectations, collective motivation, and intra- and inter-temporal agency.

Here, sentiment is reconceptualized as a multidimensional state variable encompassing financial markets mood, demographic structure, and sociocultural confidence. In this broader sense, sentiment governs not only market volatility or risk aversion, but also the willingness of societies to invest in futures they cannot yet observe. Demographic energy, institutional trust, and social narratives of progress all enter into the architecture of growth, modulating both the supply of innovation finance and its productivity. This deepened understanding allows us to reinterpret growth divergence, stagnation traps, and development failures as emergent outcomes of sentiment regimes—sentiment-driven equilibria that shape the trajectory of economic potential across generations.

Standard macroeconomic accounts of long-run growth focus on the accumulation of capital, labor, and technology. In endogenous growth models, innovation and productivity are modeled as the result of deliberate investments with high future returns. Yet across time and space, economies with similar structural endowments often display radically different growth trajectories. These divergences cannot be fully explained by material factors alone. In the SAGE framework, such asymmetries are traced to a deeper layer: the **sentiment configuration** of an economy—a state-dependent, multidimensional variable that governs how agents perceive the future, form expectations, assign utility, and act under uncertainty.

This section expands the concept of sentiment beyond financial mood or market risk appetite, situating it as a systemic and socially embedded determinant of growth. In the long run, sentiment encompasses not only expectations and beliefs, but also demographic energy, collective motivation, intertemporal imagination, and the cultural disposition toward risk and change. It is through this broader lens that growth trajectories and their bifurcations are reinterpreted in the SAGE model.

In earlier sections, variable ϖ_t has been defined as a forward-looking, sentiment-based rational-expectations variable that influences the marginal utility of assets with varying liquidity, price volatility, and duration. While this formulation remains here central, over longer horizons, ϖ_t must be understood more broadly—not merely as a statistical expectations or pricing kernel, but as an aggregate disposition of people toward the future.

Let us define the long-run sentiment state as:

$$\varpi_t = \varpi_t^{fin} \cdot \varpi_t^{soc} \cdot \varpi_t^{demo},$$

where:

- $\mathfrak{o}_t^{fin}$: financial market sentiment (risk preferences, liquidity premia),
- $\mathfrak{o}_t^{soc}$: social-cultural sentiment (trust in institutions, societal cohesion, perceived agency),
- $\mathfrak{o}_t^{demo}$: demographic sentiment (energy, optimism, willingness to act embedded in population structure).

This generalized sentiment variable $\mathfrak{o}_t$ affects both innovation efficiency and asset valuation in the long term. In particular, it determines how much of society's potential is activated through capital allocation, institutional innovation, and social risk-taking.

Sentiment-Driven Growth Dynamics
To integrate sentiment into the growth engine of the economy, using Eqs. (4.6) and (4.8), define endogenous growth as the product of capital allocation, capital efficiency, and productivity, each modulated by sentiment:

$$g_t = \varrho_{K.t}(\mathfrak{o}_t)k_tA_t(\mathfrak{o}_t, \psi_t)\mathcal{W}.$$

This formulation embeds sentiment in both wealth allocation to capital (via $\varrho_{K.\ t}$) and productivity (via A_t).One natural specification for TFP is:

$$A_t(\mathfrak{o}_t, \psi_t) = A^0\ exp\left[-a_1\xi_{K,t} - a_2\sigma_{K,t} + a_3\mathfrak{o}_t^{demo}\right],$$

where A^0 is baseline TFP and the exponential term captures the effect of capital's liquidation cost $\xi_{K,\ t}$ and price volatility $\sigma_{K,\ t}$, and demographic sentiment $\mathfrak{o}_t^{demo}$ on the effectiveness of innovation. Regarding the latter, an aging, mistrustful, and pessimistic society leads to a low-innovation, low-growth regime, while a young, cohesive, and forward-looking one generates high investment in risky innovation and supports a high-growth regime.

Portfolio Allocations and Growth Feedback
Sentiment also affects growth through its impact on portfolio choices. Households dynamically allocate wealth across assets based on perceived risk and expected returns. The effective share of capital in the wealth portfolio is given by $\varrho_{K,t} = \frac{K_t}{\Delta\varepsilon_{K,t}(\mathfrak{o}_t)}\frac{1}{\mathcal{W}}$.

One specification for $\varrho_{K,\ t}$ is:

$$\varrho_{K,t}(\mathfrak{o}_t) = \varrho_K^0\exp\left[-r_1\xi_{K,t} - r_2\sigma_{K,t} + r_3\mathfrak{o}_t^{fin}\mathfrak{o}_t^{soc}\mathfrak{o}_t^{demo}\right].$$

Here, $\mathfrak{o}_t^{fin}$, $\mathfrak{o}_t^{soc}$ and $\mathfrak{o}_t^{demo}$ combine to amplify or dampen the marginal utility of holding capital. The former type of sentiment—financial market sentiment—depends on factors like the prevailing mood in financial markets, risk tolerance, expectations about macroeconomic and monetary policy conditions. On the other hand, social sentiment reflects collective trust in institutions, perceptions of fairness and cohesion, and the societal willingness to undertake long-term transformation.

Furthermore, demographic sentiment changes with such factors as, inter alia, population growth, age composition, dependency, health, migration patterns—all factors that influence not just the growth potential of the economy but also people's perceptions of that potential. As $\varrho_{K,\ t}$ rises—due to positive sentiments—capital accumulation accelerates, the effectiveness of capital improves, and the growth rate of the economy increases. This introduces a feedback loop: sentiment affects capital allocation, which in turn affects capital deployment and, hence, future output growth.

Such effects are difficult to capture in standard models. Yet they emerge naturally in SAGE's utility structure once sentiment is introduced and understood broadly, as discussed above. The result is a powerful, endogenous mechanism through which financial, social, and demographic variables become inputs into the long-run economic growth process through intra- and inter-temporal resource allocation choices made by rational *and* sentient human beings.

SAGE suggests that long-run growth trajectories are sentiment-sensitive. Optimism embedded in demographic and institutional beliefs raises capital efficiency, accelerates innovation, and promotes investment behavior. The endogenous interaction between sentiment, capital productivity, and resource allocation allows for different growth regimes. SAGE, thus, endogenizes growth potential as a function of belief regimes, extending beyond traditional fundamentals. It provides a structural rationale for why some economies stagnate despite stable investment-to-GDP ratios, while others achieve sustained take-offs driven by sentiment-fueled innovation cycles. This approach helps unify behavioral and macro-financial insights into a coherent theory of long-run economic development.

4.11 Labor Force Participation

Standard macroeconomic models explain labor force participation dynamics through static incentives—mainly the interplay between wages, taxes, and benefits—or through frictions affecting the unemployed. SAGE departs from this view by modeling labor supply as a forward-looking, utility-maximizing decision, in which households consider not only current wages but the expected job value *JV*, shaped by rational expectations influenced by sentiment dynamics. This yields new insights into why prime-age labor force participation may decline even without a collapse in real wages, particularly in post-crisis environments characterized by persistent pessimism.

As derived in Appendix E, households compute the present value of working by evaluating the expected discounted stream of returns from labor, net of disutility, adjusted for the perceived risk of job loss and real wage erosion. Let the job value at time t, conditional on prevailing sentiment, be denoted by:

$$JV_t(\mathbb{o}_t) = \sum_{\tau=1}^{\infty} \beta^t \mathbb{E}_t \left[(1 - u_{t+\tau}) w_{t+\tau} - \chi \frac{L_{t+\tau}^{1-\nu}}{1+\nu} \right], \tag{4.14}$$

where $u_{t+\tau}$ is the probability of the agent finding herself unemployed at date $t + \tau$, with $\tau \in (1, \infty)$, and w is the rale wage rate, and $\chi \frac{L_{t+\tau}^{1-\nu}}{1+\nu}$ is disutility of labor, increasing and convex in labor supply. Equation (4.14), thus, represents the dynamic utility flow from working, net of labor disutility, adjusted for future employment probability, and discounted over time.

In SAGE, JV_t is an endogenous valuation of labor, functioning much like a long-duration asset whose future yield stream is discounted not just by time, but by beliefs about future wage stability and employment risk. This conceptualization allows to reinterpret labor participation behavior as a rational response to asset revaluation in the household's lifetime utility-maximization problem.

Households choose labor supply L_t to equate the marginal disutility of labor with the marginal utility of consumption financed by expected job value. Using the reduced-form utility function from Sect. 3.2, here report for reader's convenience:

$$U_t = \log(C_t) + \theta_M(\mathbb{o}_t) \log(M_t) + \theta_B(\mathbb{o}_t) \log(B_t) + \theta_K(\mathbb{o}_t) \log(K_t) - \chi \frac{L_{t+\tau}^{1-\nu}(\mathbb{o}_t)}{1+\nu}.$$

Optimality requires:

$$\chi L_t^{\nu}(\mathbb{o}_t) = \frac{1}{C_t} JV_t(\mathbb{o}_t).$$

This implies that labor supply depends positively on job value. In optimistic sentiment states, JV_t is high due to expectations of stable employment and wage growth, encouraging participation. Conversely, under pessimistic sentiment, households assign low expected value to future labor income and discount it heavily due to elevated unemployment risk and wage uncertainty. Even if observed wages have not declined, this endogenous drop in JV_t leads to a rational reduction in labor supply, and possibly labor force exit, particularly among marginal or discouraged workers.

These dynamics reveal a distinct macro-behavioral channel absent in standard search-theoretic models: sentiment-driven withdrawals from the labor force by currently employed workers. The participation decision is no longer exclusively a function of current job offers or market frictions, but also a function of how households perceive the future value of remaining in the labor market.

Let the household face a participation threshold JV^C, such that:

$$L_t^* > 0 \Leftrightarrow JV_t \geq JV^C,$$

that is, in equilibrium, a household will participate in the labor market (i.e., choose a strictly positive optimal labor supply if and only if the perceived job value exceeds or equals a threshold value).

When $JV_t < JV^C$, the household optimally exits the labor force—even preemptively. This mechanism explains puzzling empirical features of the post-2008 period noted in some advanced economies, including:

- The decline in participation among prime-age workers despite recovering GDP and stable wages.
- The shift toward self-employment, early retirement, or home production among individuals who were previously employed.
- The coexistence of rising job vacancies and stagnant labor force growth, consistent with sentiment-based revaluations of job attractiveness.

In SAGE, participation and portfolio allocation are jointly determined. As JV_t declines due to pessimistic sentiment, the perceived marginal value of labor income contracts. This triggers three reinforcing portfolio shifts:

1. **Decline in labor supply** reduces expected income streams and dampens consumption demand.
2. **Rise in the marginal utility of liquidity** lowers expected labor income and increases precautionary demand for liquid assets, such as money M_t and bonds B_t, which offer safety and immediate access to real resources (notably consumption).
3. **Decline in capital allocation** lowers expected income and job stability reduce households' willingness to hold illiquid and volatile assets such as equity capital K_t.

Formally, under the optimal household program, it can be observed that:

$$\frac{\partial L_t^*}{\partial \omega_t} > 0, \frac{\partial M_t^*}{\partial \omega_t} < 0, \frac{\partial K_t^*}{\partial \omega_t} > 0.$$

Thus, declining sentiment depresses both labor supply and risk-taking, creating a behaviorally consistent reallocation of effort and wealth. Job value is thus not merely an input into the labor-leisure decision, but part of a broader rebalancing across human and financial capital, which is sensitive to sentiment and liquidity conditions.

This integration reveals the deep structural link between the perceived value of work and the demand for financial assets. Households holding gloomy views about their employment future rationally pivot to liquid saving, reduce their exposure to long-term assets (including human capital), and exit the labor force. The result is a dual withdrawal: from labor markets and from investment, both of which contribute negatively to the economy and entrench pessimism.

This participation mechanism is not macroeconomically neutral. It introduces a self-reinforcing loop, which from negative sentiment runs to even more negative sentiment, through lower job value, lower labor supply, lower aggregate output, and lower wages.

This loop reflects rational expectations-consistent utility maximization, not irrational behavior. It supports persistent low-output, low-participation equilibria in the absence of structural shocks or nominal rigidities, paralleling the stagnation regime discussed in Sect. 4.2. As with capital demand, the response of labor supply to sentiment exhibits downward asymmetry: exit from the labor force is faster than re-entry, and once households drop out, the ability to rejoin declines due to decayed skills, weaker job networks, and further reductions in JV_t.

As noted, this mechanism helps explain several real-world anomalies. In the United States, the long secular decline in labor force participation among prime-age men accelerated significantly after the 2008 crisis and again during the COVID19 pandemic. Similarly, prime-age female participation, after decades of growth, has recently plateaued and slightly reversed despite rising education levels and policy support. In many advanced economies, jobless recoveries and persistent participation gaps followed financial shocks, even as employment-to-population ratios failed to recover pre-crisis trends. These patterns are difficult to reconcile with models focused solely on wage or tax disincentives but are consistent with a decline in perceived job value, as formalized in SAGE.

4.12 Sentiment and Inflation

SAGE can be used to show how a sharp deterioration in the sentiment variable ω_t can trigger inflation through the **Portfolio Theory of Inflation (PTI)** channel.[11] This section applies SAGE to an open economy and formalizes the effect of a confidence crisis on inflation. To keep the analysis simple, the focus here shifts from global investors (as in the original PTI formulation) to a representative domestic household, who reallocates wealth across asset classes in response to changing beliefs about monetary and macroeconomic stability. Although certain key results of the PTI cannot be captured using this simplified framework—particularly regarding the market power that global investors exert on domestic economies compared to local households—this model sufficiently demonstrates how inflation can arise from agents adjusting their portfolios in response to changes in sentiment.

To accommodate an open economy, let us introduce the nominal exchange rate e_t (units of domestic currency per unit of foreign currency), foreign currency-denominated assets F_t, and tradable consumption priced at P_t^C, which is influenced by both domestic and imported prices. Here, F is a reserve currency and acts as a safe-haven asset during confidence crises; therefore, $\frac{\partial \Delta \varepsilon_{F,t}(\omega_t)}{\partial \omega_t} < 0$, while $\frac{\partial \Delta \varepsilon_{a,t}(\omega_t)}{\partial \omega_t} > 0$, for $a \in \{M, B, K\}$.

Modifying Eqs. (3.6) and (3.9) accordingly, the representative domestic household maximizes expected lifetime utility:

[11] For a comprehensive discussion of the PTI, see Bossone (2025), Chap. 13, cit.

$$U(C_t, M_t, B_t, K_t, L_t; \mathbb{o}_t) = log\, C_t + \theta_M(\mathbb{o}_t)\, log\left(\frac{M_t}{P_{C,t}C_t}\right)$$
$$+ \theta_B(\mathbb{o}_t)\, log\left(\frac{P_{B,t}B_t}{P_{C,t}C_t[1 + \xi_{B,t}(\mathbb{o}_t) + \sigma_{B,t}(\mathbb{o}_t)]}\right)$$
$$+ \theta_K(\mathbb{o}_t)\, log\left(\frac{P_{K,t}K_t}{P_{C,t}C_t[1 + \xi_{K,t}(\mathbb{o}_t) + \sigma_{K,t}(\mathbb{o}_t)]}\right)$$
$$+ \theta_F(\mathbb{o}_t)\, log\left(\frac{e_t F_t}{P_{C,t}C_t[1 + \xi_{F,t}(\mathbb{o}_t) + \sigma_{F,t}(\mathbb{o}_t)]}\right) - \chi\frac{L_t^{1-\nu}(\mathbb{o}_t)}{1+\nu} \tag{4.15}$$

subject to the intertemporal budget constraint:

$$P_{C,t}C_t \leq M_t + \Delta M_{H,t} + P_{B,t}B_t + P_{K,t}K_t + e_t F_t + \mathbb{E}_0 \sum_{t=0}^{\infty} \mathbb{E}_t[y_t|\mathbb{o}_t]$$
$$+ r^n_{B,t-1}P_{B_{t-1}}B_{t-1} + r^n_{K,t-1}P_{K,t-1}K_{t-1} + M_{t-1} - r^n_{M,t-1}\Delta M_{H,t-1}$$
$$+ e_{t-1}r^n_{F,t-1}F_{t-1}. \tag{4.16}$$

Assume that, as in any open economy, consumption includes imported goods, with share γ. The consumer price index is then given by:

$$P_{C,t} = (P_{C_D,t})^{1-\gamma}(e_t P_{F,t})^{\gamma} \tag{4.17}$$

where subscripts D and F stand for domestic and foreign, respectively.

The first-order conditions of plan (4.15)–(4.17) are:

$$\frac{1}{C_t} = \lambda_t$$
$$\frac{\theta_M(\mathbb{o}_t)}{M_t} = \lambda_t \Longrightarrow M_t = \theta_M(\mathbb{o}_t)C_t$$
$$\frac{\theta_B(\mathbb{o}_t)}{B_t} = \lambda_t P_{C,t}\Delta\varepsilon_{B,t}(\mathbb{o}_t)$$
$$\frac{\theta_K(\mathbb{o}_t)}{K_t} = \lambda_t P_{C,t}\Delta\varepsilon_{K,t}(\mathbb{o}_t)$$
$$\frac{\theta_F(\mathbb{o}_t)}{e_{F,t}F_t} = \lambda_t P_{C,t}\Delta\varepsilon_{F,t}(\mathbb{o}_t).$$

These conditions define a sentiment-contingent portfolio allocation; that is, they determine the optimal portfolio allocation given the household's preferences and rational expectations on asset liquidation costs and price volatility, as influenced by sentiment. Note that the demand for money is proportional to consumption, scaled by a sentiment-sensitive coefficient $\theta_M(\mathbb{o}_t)$. A fall in sentiment leads to a decline in θ_M, θ_B and θ_K, and a rise in θ_F, thereby reducing the household's desired holdings of money, bonds and capital, and triggering an endogenous reallocation toward goods and foreign currency.

Inflation as a Portfolio Adjustment Outcome
From the money demand condition:

$$M_t = \theta_M(\mathbb{o}_t)C_t \Rightarrow \frac{P_{C,t}}{M_t} = \frac{1}{\theta_M(\mathbb{o}_t)} \frac{C_t}{P_{C,t}}.$$

Assuming nominal money supply $\overline{M}$ is fixed (or grows exogenously), the price level adjusts to equate money demand and supply. Taking logs and first differences, and rearranging:

$$p_{C,t} = \Delta\, log\, C_t - \Delta\, log\, \overline{M}_t - \Delta\, log\, \theta_M(\mathbb{o}_t),$$

where $p_{C,\,t}$ is the rate of change of $P_{C,\,t}$, that is, the rate of inflatiom. Notice that even if $\overline{M}_t$is constant, a decline in $\theta_M(\mathbb{o}_t)$, which reflects a sentiment decline, causes both consumption and inflation to rise. When confidence falls, agents reallocate their wealth away from money, raising the price level.

Foreign currency-denominated assets and the exchange rate provide an additional transmission mechanism. With F_t included in the portfolio, if $\mathbb{o}_t$ declines, the demand for the foreign currency θ_F rises, and the FX market adjusts via nominal depreciation, i.e., e_t increases. If consumption includes imported goods, from Eq. (4.17) follows:

$$\Delta\, log\, P_{C,t} \approx p_{C,t} = (1-\gamma)p_{C_D,t} + \gamma - \Delta\, log\, e_t,$$

which shows that depreciation amplifies inflation through imported goods prices, with its impact growing with the degree of openness of the economy. The inflation process becomes self-fulfilling, detached from fundamentals or policy decisions. Even tightening monetary policy may fail to reverse these dynamics if confidence is not restored.

This open-economy extension of SAGE demonstrates how a sentiment-driven resource reallocation by a representative domestic household can endogenously generate inflation. The confidence collapse, captured as a fall in $\mathbb{o}_t$, triggers a shift away from money and toward goods and foreign currency, destabilizing the price level through the portfolio channel. This yields inflation without any monetary or fiscal stimulus, purely as a consequence of shifting beliefs about the future value of nominal holdings.

By grounding the PTI mechanism in a general equilibrium structure with recursive sentiment, this model captures sentiment-contingent inflation regimes and shows how monetary policy effectiveness depends critically on the public's confidence in the institutional and policy framework—rather than on policy instruments alone.

4.13 Demographics, Intergenerational Sentiment, and OLG Extensions

The final section of this chapter extends the SAGE framework to a two-period overlapping generations (OLG) structure, introducing demographic heterogeneity and intergenerational sentiment dynamics into the model.

Each agent lives for two periods: in the first period, the agent works, consumes, and allocates savings across assets; in the second period, the agent retires and consumes from the proceeds of liquidating previously acquired assets. This structure enables the modeling of generational beliefs formation, intertemporal sentiment propagation, and age-dependent portfolio behavior. The OLG-SAGE formulation maintains tractability while enhancing realism, allowing the model to capture persistent sentiment-based stagnation, sentiment hysteresis, and demographic amplifiers of macro-financial dynamics. The section develops the household problem, defines cohort sentiment dynamics, and derives aggregate equilibrium conditions under intergenerational heterogeneity.

The representative-agent structure in baseline SAGE abstracts from life-cycle features such as working-age income, retirement, and generational turnover. Yet these aspects are central to real-world economic behavior and beliefs formation. Different generations are exposed to different economic events, institutional regimes, and social narratives, which shape their expectations, trust in institutions, and portfolio preferences. Incorporating an OLG structure enables SAGE to formalize how historical experience, sentiment memory, and intergenerational trust dynamics affect economic outcomes.

The OLG extension provides:

- Life-cycle heterogeneity in portfolio allocation,
- Intergenerational propagation of sentiment,
- A structural explanation for belief hysteresis,
- Demographic determinants of long-run stagnation or exuberance.

These extensions align with SAGE's core commitment to modeling sentiment as an endogenous state variable co-evolving with reason, information, and changing macroeconomic conditions.

Household Optimization in a Two-Period Life
Agents live for two periods. In period 1 (young), they work, earn wage income, consume, and allocate wealth across money M, bonds B, and capital K. In period 2 (old), they consume using the proceeds from asset liquidation. The agent's utility function is:

$$U = u\left(C_t^y, M_t, B_t, K_t, L_t; \mathbb{o}_t\right) = \beta \mathbb{E}_t\left[u\left(C_{t+1}^0; \mathbb{o}_{t+1}\right)\right]$$

subject to

$$P_{C,t}C_t^y + M_t + P_{B,t}B_t + P_{K,t}K_t = w_t L_t$$

and

$$P_{C,t+1}C_{t+1}^y = \sum_{a \in \{M,B,K\}} \frac{1}{1 + \xi_{a,t}(\mathbb{o}_t) + \sigma_{a,t}(\mathbb{o}_t)} P_{a,t}a_t.$$

The young agent chooses $C_t^y, M_t, B_t, K_t, L_t$ to maximize utility. The first-order conditions for each asset $a \in \{M, B, K\}$ are:

$$\frac{\partial u}{\partial a_t} = \beta \mathbb{E}_t\left[\frac{1}{1 + \xi_{a,t}(\mathbb{o}_t) + \sigma_{a,t}(\mathbb{o}_t)} \frac{P_{a,t+1}}{P_{C,t+1}} \frac{\partial u}{\partial C_{t+1}^o}\right], \tag{4.18}$$

which captures the intertemporal trade-off between allocating income toward current consumption versus future consumption mediated by expected asset returns, adjusted for sentiment-contingent liquidation costs and price volatility. Equation (4.18) allows sentiment to influence the future expected asset risk-return profile, generating feedback loops where negative sentiment amplifies risk perceptions, which in turn suppresses investment and reinforces pessimism.

Sentiment Dynamics Across Generations

Let $\mathbb{o}_t^y$ and $\mathbb{o}_t^o$ represent sentiment in period t for young and old agents, respectively. Aggregate sentiment $\mathbb{o}_t$ is:

$$\mathbb{o}_t = \delta_t \mathbb{o}_t^y + (1 - \delta_t)\mathbb{o}_t^o,$$

where $\delta_t = \frac{N_t^y}{N_t^y + N_t^o}$ reflects the relative demographic share of young agents. Old-age sentiment may differ from youth sentiment. Let sentiment evolve according to:

$$\mathbb{o}_t^o = \mu_t \mathbb{o}_{t-1}^y + (1 - \mu_t)\mathbb{o}_t',$$

with $\mu \in (0, 1)$ representing sentiment memory and $\mathbb{o}_t'$ is an exogenous sentiment update from news or public signals. Sentiment updating for new cohorts depends on available information Ω concerning, macro conditions, expected developments, and social narratives, all filtered by agents' knowledge. The sentiment-contingent rational expectations evolve as:

$$\mathbb{K}_t = \mu_t \mathbb{K}_{t-1} + (1 - \mu_t)\mathbb{k}(\Omega_t),$$

where the updating function $\mathbb{k}(\cdot)$ maps contemporaneous information into expectation revisions, and the dynamics of Ω are discussed in Appendix B. This kernel provides a tractable way to model intergenerational transmission of sentiment, anchoring cohort-specific behavior in both inherited information and new interpretive signals. A high μ indicates expectations inertia and generational memory.

The structure defined here admits tractable analytical and numerical solutions under standard functional forms. Future work may calibrate or simulate the full model to explore transitional dynamics and comparative statics under demographic shocks (see Chap. 6).

Aggregation and General Equilibrium
The SAGE framework remains in place with the following adjustments:

- Labor is supplied only by the young.
- Consumption demand and portfolio allocations differ by age.
- Price formation reflects cohort-weighted sentiment.

Market-clearing conditions:

Goods : $Y_t = C_t^y + C_t^o + I_t + G_t$
Assets : $M_t + B_t + K_t = A_t^y + A_t^o$
Labor : $L_t = L_t^y$.

Cohort-specific asset demands determine the aggregate portfolio allocation. Asset utility weights are given by:

$$\theta_{a,t} = \frac{\partial u(C_t^y, M_t, B_t, K_t, L_t; \mathbb{o}_t)}{\partial a_t} \Big/ \frac{\partial u(C_t^y, M_t, B_t, K_t, L_t; \mathbb{o}_t)}{\partial C_t^y}.$$

Implications and Interpretive Power
This OLG extension enhances SAGE in several directions:

- **Sentiment-driven secular stagnation**: Persistently pessimistic cohorts, shaped by crisis events or narratives of decline, tend to adopt conservative portfolio strategies—hoarding liquid assets, avoiding risk, and refraining from productive investment. As these cohorts age and gain wealth, their preferences weigh more heavily on aggregate asset demand, reducing the effective natural interest rate. This drives the economy toward stagnation equilibria (discussed in Sect. 4.2) characterized by low investment, subdued inflation, and diminished innovation.
- **Demographic financial cycles**: As demographic transitions unfold—e.g., baby booms aging into retirement—the aggregate sentiment becomes more liquidity-preferring and less tolerant of risk. Older generations prefer capital preservation, pushing up demand for safe assets and depressing yields. These shifts can generate endogenous financial cycles: a youthful, risk-taking phase followed by

a mature, conservative phase that flattens yield curves and reduces monetary transmission potency.

- **Cohort memory effects**: Economic experiences during formative years create durable imprints on belief structures. A generation exposed to high inflation or financial instability retains heightened perceptions of volatility and distrust in financial markets, which shape their decisions even decades later. This memory persistence embeds past shocks into future macro dynamics and explains sluggish recovery or enduring risk aversion.
- **Cross-country heterogeneity**: In open economies, generational structures and memory profiles vary by country. Nations with recent crises may be dominated by cautious cohorts, while others may host optimistic, risk-tolerant young populations. These cross-sectional differences in sentiment lead to capital flow imbalances, divergent interest rate paths, and dissimilar policy effectiveness, even under similar structural fundamentals.
- **Demographic feedbacks**: Shifts in the age distribution alter the weight of different sentiment profiles in aggregate belief formation. A growing elderly population increases the influence of older generations' sentiment on asset pricing and macro outcomes. This demographic drift may attenuate the impact of optimistic young cohorts, inducing a form of endogenous inertia that slows recovery or neutralizes policy interventions.
- **Hysteresis and path dependence**: Once a negative sentiment equilibrium takes hold—especially in large or wealthy cohorts—it can persist via intergenerational influence or institutional reinforcement. The economy becomes stuck in a self-validating loop where low expectations reduce investment, confirm pessimism, and perpetuate stagnation. This dynamic offers a structural foundation for persistent output gaps, secular stagnation, and low responsiveness to conventional stimulus.
- **Age-structured policy impact**: Monetary or fiscal policies may affect generations differently. For instance, rate cuts may encourage young borrowing but penalize old savers, leading to muted aggregate effects. Similarly, stimulus targeting asset prices may disproportionately benefit older, asset-rich cohorts. The OLG-SAGE framework makes it possible to trace these differential effects and to design policies that consider cohort-specific sensitivities.
- **Sentiment conflicts and coordination traps**: When generational sentiment diverges sharply, economic agents may interpret signals differently, fail to coordinate on shared expectations, and undermine policy credibility. Young optimists and old pessimists may react in opposing directions to the same stimulus, leading to muted or erratic aggregate behavior. Such dissonance raises the likelihood of policy failure, instability, or delayed adjustment.
- **Wealth distribution and asset pricing**: If older cohorts hold a dominant share of financial assets, their sentiment preferences will disproportionately shape asset prices. Even if younger generations are more optimistic, they may lack the market power to move prices. This asymmetry creates a wedge between underlying economic potential and actual investment behavior, driving mispricing, low capital formation, and skewed intertemporal resource allocation.

These implications make the OLG-SAGE framework especially well-suited for analyzing macro-financial developments in aging societies, persistent low-rate environments, and sentiment-fragmented economies, especially well-suited for analyzing macro-financial developments in aging societies, persistent low-rate environments, and sentiment-fragmented economies.

In conclusion, the OLG extension to SAGE preserves analytical tractability while significantly enriching its descriptive and explanatory power. By allowing sentiment to vary across age cohorts and persist over time, and to affect portfolio allocation choices based on age generation-related preferences, the model captures essential dimensions of real-world macro-financial dynamics. The resulting OLG-SAGE framework can accommodate multiple sentiment equilibria, demographic shifts, and intergenerational belief cycles—offering a compelling platform for policy analysis in aging, uncertain, and memory-rich economies. Future developments may incorporate endogenous retirement, bequests, and fertility choices linked to sentiment, deepening the theory's capacity to explain structural stagnation and sentiment-driven growth divergence.

Having applied SAGE to a broad spectrum of macroeconomic phenomena, the next chapter explores the power of SAGE in a historical context by applying it to a retrospective thought experiment.

References

Aghion, P., & Howitt, P. (1992). A model of growth through creative destruction. *Econometrica, 60* (2), 323–351.

Alfaro, L., Kalemli-Ozcan, S., & Volosovych, V. (2008). Why doesn't capital flow from rich to poor countries? An empirical investigation. *Review of Economics and Statistics, 90*(2), 347–368.

Bernanke, B. S. (2005, March 10). *The global saving glut and the U.S. current account deficit.* Remarks by Governor Bernanke at the Sandridge Lecture, Virginia Association of Economists.

Bossone, B. (2025). *Trailblazing visions of money in economic theory: Essence, genesis, and economic ramifications* (Contributions to economics). Springer Nature Switzerland AG.

Broner, F., Didier, T., Erce, A., & Schmukler, S. (2013). Gross capital flows: Dynamics and crises. *Journal of Monetary Economics, 60*(1), 113–133.

Brunnermeier, M. K., & Sannikov, Y. (2014). A macroeconomic model with a financial sector. *American Economic Review, 104*(2), 379–421.

Caballero, R. J., Farhi, E., & Gourinchas, P. O. (2008). An equilibrium model of "global imbalances" and low interest rates. *American Economic Review, 98*(1), 358–393.

Calvo, G. A. (1998). Capital flows and capital-market crises: The simple economics of sudden stops. *Journal of Applied Economics, 1*, 35.

Calvo, G. A., Izquierdo, A., & Mejía, L. F. (2004). *On the empirics of sudden stops: The relevance of balance-sheet effects.* NBER Working Paper No. 10520, National Bureau of Economic Research. American Economic Review, Papers and Proceedings.

Dornbusch, R. (1976). Expectations and exchange rate dynamics. *Journal of Political Economy, 84* (6), 1161–1176.

Eggertsson, G. B., & Mehrotra, N. R. (2014). *A model of secular stagnation.* NBER Working Paper No. 20574(October). National Bureau of Economic Research.

Farmer, R. E. A. (2012). The evolution of endogenous business cycles. *Macroeconomic Dynamics, 16*(S2), 227–252.

Geanakoplos, J. (2010). The leverage cycle. In *NBER Macroeconomics Annual 2009* (Vol. 24, pp. 1–65). National Bureau of Economic Research.

Gourinchas, P. O., & Jeanne, O. (2013). Capital flows to developing countries: The allocation puzzle. *The Review of Economic Studies, 80*(4), 1484–1515.

Gourinchas, P. O., & Rey, H. (2014). External adjustment, global imbalances, valuation effects. In G. Gita, E. Helpman, & K. Rogoff (Eds.), *Handbook of international economics* (Vol. 4, pp. 585–645). Elsevier.

Ju, J., & Wei, S. J. (2010). Domestic institutions and the bypass effect of financial globalization. *American Economic Journal: Economic Policy, 2*(4), 173–204.

Lettau, M., & Ludvigson, S. C. (2001). Consumption, aggregate wealth, and expected stock returns. *Journal of Finance, 56*(3), 815–849.

Lucas, R. E., Jr. (1990). Why doesn't capital flow from rich to poor countries? *American Economic Review, 80*(2), 92–96.

Mehra, R., & Prescott, E. C. (1985). The equity premium: A puzzle. *Journal of Monetary Economics, 15*(2), 145–161.

Mendoza, E. G. (2002). Credit, prices, and crashes: Business cycles with a sudden stop. In *NBER Macroeconomics Annual 2002*. MIT Press.

Phelps, E. S. (2009). *Structural slumps: The modern equilibrium theory of unemployment, interest, and assets*. Harvard University Press.

Romer, P. M. (1990). Endogenous technological change. *Journal of Political Economy, 98*(5, Part 2), S71–S102.

Summers, L. H. (2014). U.S. economic prospects: Secular stagnation, hysteresis, and the zero lower bound. *Business Economics, 49*(2), 65–73.

Chapter 5
Could SAGE Have Anticipated the 2007–09 Global Financial Crisis?

Abstract This chapter applies SAGE to a retrospective thought experiment: could the 2007–09 global financial crisis have been foreseen using the framework's logic? It argues that key features of the crisis—such as liquidity-hoarding, asset fire sales, and investment collapse—can be understood as equilibrium responses to deteriorating sentiment and shifting expectations. The model shows how sentiment-contingent portfolio rebalancing can trigger self-reinforcing pessimism, with even small shocks generating major macro-financial consequences when trust erodes and liquidity evaporates. The chapter highlights how conventional models missed these dynamics by treating sentiment as exogenous or irrational. In contrast, SAGE formalizes sentiment as a rationally grounded yet unstable driver of expectations, capable of amplifying perceived uncertainty into systemic fragility. It illustrates how worsening sentiment undermined the perceived utility of illiquid assets and increased the demand for money, creating financial bottlenecks. By capturing the feedback loop between sentiment, expectations, and portfolio behavior, SAGE offers a structured and microfounded explanation of crisis propagation. The chapter suggests that applying SAGE ex ante could have helped identify vulnerabilities in the lead-up to the crisis—not through forecasting shocks, but by recognizing sentiment-contingent tipping points embedded in market psychology and institutional fragility.

This chapter undertakes a thought experiment: had the SAGE framework been available prior to 2007, could it have provided early warnings of the impending global financial crisis—not by forecasting its precise timing, but by revealing the endogenous fragility of the pre-crisis configuration?

Rather than applying the model retrospectively in a deterministic sense, let us explore how the core mechanisms of SAGE—the endogeneity of sentiment, its effect on asset valuation, and the nonlinear dynamics of portfolio reallocation—could have uncovered the structural incompatibility of prevailing beliefs with macroeconomic stability. The objective is not historical re-engineering but theoretical illumination: to assess whether, in principle, a SAGE-informed analytical lens would have flagged the crisis-prone nature of the financial system in real time.

B. Bossone, *Bringing Sentiment into Economic Reason*, SpringerBriefs in Economics, https://doi.org/10.1007/978-3-032-08617-4_5

Sentiment-Driven Overinvestment and the Fragility of Capital Allocation
In SAGE, sentiment $\mathbb{O}_t$ shapes the perceived utility efficiency of different assets differently. Specifically, the utility contribution of capital is inversely related to its expected illiquidity and volatility, both of which are sentiment-contingent. Replicating here Eq. (3.6):

$$U(C_t, M_t, B_t, K_t, L_t; \mathbb{O}_t) = log\, C_t + \theta_M(\mathbb{O}_t)\, log\left(\frac{M_t}{P_t C_t}\right)$$
$$+ \theta_B(\mathbb{O}_t)\, log\left(\frac{P_{B,t} B_t}{P_t C_t\left[1 + \xi_{B,t}(\mathbb{O}_t) + \sigma_{B,t}(\mathbb{O}_t)\right]}\right)$$
$$+ \theta_K(\mathbb{O}_t)\, log\left(\frac{P_{K,t} K_t}{P_t C_t\left[1 + \xi_{K,t}(\mathbb{O}_t) + \sigma_{K,t}(\mathbb{O}_t)\right]}\right) - \chi \frac{L_t^{1-\nu}(\mathbb{O}_t)}{1+\nu},$$

and recalling that asset K is illiquid and its price volatile, one has:

$$\frac{\partial \xi_{K_t}}{\partial \mathbb{O}_t}, \frac{\partial \sigma_{K_t}}{\partial \mathbb{O}_t} < 0, \lim_{\mathbb{O}_t \to +\infty} \xi_{K_t} \to \xi^*_{K_t}, \quad \lim_{\mathbb{O}_t \to +\infty} \sigma_{K_t} \to \sigma^*_{K_t}, \quad \lim_{\mathbb{O}_t \to 0} \xi_{K_t} \to \overline{\xi}_{K_t}$$
$$\gg \xi^*_{K_t} \lim_{\mathbb{O}_t \to 0} \sigma_{K_t} \to \overline{\sigma}_{K_t} \gg \sigma^*_{K_t},$$

where $\xi^*_{K_t}$ and $\sigma^*_{K_t}$ indicate, respectively, K's minimum liquidation cost and price volatility, consistent with the economy's financial structure, when $\mathbb{O}_t = 1$ (see Sect. 3.1).[1]

During the pre-crisis period (2003–2006), a confluence of asset price inflation, abundant global liquidity, regulatory leniency, and a prevailing belief in the self-stabilizing nature of financial markets pushed $\mathbb{O}_t$ toward persistently high values. Under these conditions, the perceived volatility penalty on capital assets and their liquidation costs fell to minimum levels, artificially inflating their utility-based value. This induced overinvestment in capital-intensive, opaque, and highly leveraged

[1] In the context of very high optimism, the minimum liquidation cost $\xi^*_{K_t}$ typically applied under normal conditions may temporarily decline. This occurs because assets normally considered illiquid—such as long-term capital—become highly demanded and can be rapidly sold into a market flush with eager buyers. In effect, these assets gain temporary liquidity, at least while sentiment remains elevated. Brunnermeier and Pedersen (2009) show that liquidity is endogenous and procyclical—markets appear liquid when funding is easy and optimism prevails, but this can reverse sharply, and Gorton (2010) holds that during the pre-crisis boom, even complex mortgage assets traded like liquid instruments and became toxic after 2007—an archetype of sentiment-contingent liquidity collapse. On the same line, Borio (cit.) describes how financial cycles create misperceptions of liquidity and risk, feeding instability when the tide turns. Similarly, this euphoria-driven regime may compress price volatility $\sigma^*_{K_t}$ around a unidirectional upward trend, reflecting strong price momentum with little day-to-day fluctuation. However, both effects are sentiment-contingent illusions: once optimism fades, liquidity evaporates, liquidation costs spike, and volatility re-emerges—often violently, as prices reverse direction.

instruments—such as mortgage-backed securities—despite growing underlying risks.

Equilibria and the Latent Instability Zone

The portfolio condition balancing marginal utility per unit cost across assets implies that capital gains dominance when its adjusted efficiency exceeds that of safer assets. However, according to SAGE, this equilibrium is precariously balanced on the trajectory of sentiment. As $\mathbb{o}_t$ declines toward critical threshold $\mathbb{o}^C$, a tipping point is reached where

$$\left.\frac{\partial^2 U_t}{\partial K_t \partial \mathbb{o}_t}\right|_{\mathbb{o}_t \leq \mathbb{o}^C} < 0, \left.\left|\frac{\partial \sigma_{K_t}}{\partial \mathbb{o}_t}\right|\right|_{\mathbb{o}_t \leq \mathbb{o}^C} \gg 1. \tag{5.1}$$

Here, even a small downward revision in sentiment—e.g., triggered by localized increases in mortgage defaults—rapidly renders capital less liquid (i.e., its liquidation costs arise) and inflates its price volatility, undermining its utility contribution.

Conditions (5.1), taken together, describe SAGE's core instability mechanism. They define a **latent instability zone**, where equilibrium is dynamically unstable and macroeconomic configurations can shift dramatically even in response to minor shocks. In contrast to standard models that treat crises as exogenous, SAGE identifies this zone as endogenously emergent, structurally encoded in the feedback between sentiment and asset utility.

Crisis Amplification via the Liquidity Channel

Once $\mathbb{o}_t \leq \mathbb{o}^C$, the utility of illiquid assets collapses. Threshold $\mathbb{o}^C$ arises when the utility curvature in the sentiment dimension dominates the expected capital return adjustment, i.e., when the sign and magnitude of $\frac{\partial^2 U_t}{\partial K_t \partial \mathbb{o}_t}$ determine a sharp decline in capital's marginal utility. This makes the switch to liquidity assets rational under pessimism.[2] Households and institutions pivot rapidly toward liquid stores of value—money and short-term government bonds—whose utility efficiency now dominates K, since:

[2] As noted in Sect. 4.2, the critical threshold $\mathbb{o}^C$ is a formal bifurcation point grounded in the microfoundations of the SAGE model. It emerges endogenously from the structure of the model and corresponds to the point at which the cross-partial derivative $\frac{\partial^2 u(K_t)}{\partial K_t \partial \mathbb{o}_t}$ turns sufficiently negative to undermine the utility gain from holding capital. As sentiment deteriorates toward $\mathbb{o}^C$, the marginal utility of illiquid assets like capital declines sharply relative to that of liquid assets. Once $\mathbb{o}_t \leq \mathbb{o}^C$, households solve a corner portfolio problem in which the first-order condition for capital ceases to bind, and only the first order conditions for consumption, money and bonds remain active. Thus, $\mathbb{o}^C$ delineates a regime shift—from an interior solution to a liquidity-hoarding equilibrium—and reflects deep structural properties of the agents' utility functions under sentiment-contingent rational expectations.

$$\left.\frac{\partial M_t}{\partial \mathrm{o}_t}\right|_{\mathrm{o}_t \le \mathrm{o}^C}, \left.\frac{\partial B_t}{\partial \mathrm{o}_t}\right|_{\mathrm{o}_t \le \mathrm{o}^C} > 0, \text{and } \left.\frac{\partial K_t}{\partial \mathrm{o}_t}\right|_{\mathrm{o}_t \le \mathrm{o}^C} < 0. \tag{5.2}$$

Note that because of regime switch at o^C, for $\mathrm{o}_t \le \mathrm{o}^C$,

$$|\frac{\partial M_t}{\partial \mathrm{o}_t}||_{\mathrm{o}_t \le \mathrm{o}^C} \gg |\frac{\partial M_t}{\partial \mathrm{o}_t}||_{\mathrm{o}_t > \mathrm{o}^C}, \quad |\frac{\partial B_t}{\partial \mathrm{o}_t}||_{\mathrm{o}_t \le \mathrm{o}^C} \gg |\frac{\partial B_t}{\partial \mathrm{o}_t}||_{\mathrm{o}_t > \mathrm{o}^C}, \tag{5.3}$$
$$\left|\frac{\partial K_t}{\partial \mathrm{o}_t}\right|\Big|_{\mathrm{o}_t \le \mathrm{o}^C} \gg \left|\frac{\partial K_t}{\partial \mathrm{o}_t}\right|\Big|_{\mathrm{o}_t > \mathrm{o}^C},$$

reflecting the nonlinear sensitivity of the economy that characterizes SAGE: when agents are in a state of high pessimistic expectations, small changes in sentiment have disproportionate effects. Thus, under equilibrium conditions

$$\frac{1}{C_t} = \frac{\theta_M(\mathrm{o}_t)}{M_t} = \frac{\theta_B(\mathrm{o}_t)}{B_t} = \frac{\theta_K(\mathrm{o}_t)}{K_t}$$

and

$$P_{K_t} = \frac{\theta_K(\mathrm{o}_t)}{\lambda_t K_t \mathcal{E}_K^2(\mathrm{o}_t)},$$

the sentiment-induced flight to liquidity, which consists of a falling θ_K and simultaneously rising θ_M and θ_B, entails an investment collapse in illiquid assets and their prices, and a rush into liquidity. Notice that while a concurrent increase in saving should be expected to occur under the circumstances, what matters here is the change in the composition of saving, not its level: the economy may continue to save as much as before but agent preferences shift toward greater liquidity. Greater liquidity preference affects asset prices, even for a given level of saving, raising those of more liquid instruments—including the shadow price of money P_M—and lowering those of less liquid instruments.

Notice also that under the above regime-switch conditions captured by inequalities (5.2)–(5.3), the economy does not require large exogenous shocks to unravel. It implodes under the weight of sentiment-driven capital mispricing and the nonlinear propagation of falling confidence through portfolio channels. This endogenous amplification mechanism explains the swiftness and depth of the 2007–20009 downturn—features that conventional models could not anticipate, much less internalize.

Crucially, SAGE does not claim to offer deterministic crisis prediction. Instead, it identifies when a system has become multiplicity-prone and regime-unstable. In practical terms, this implies that policymakers equipped with SAGE could have monitored indicators like:

- The sentiment elasticity of capital price volatility $\frac{\partial \sigma_{K_t}}{\partial \mathbb{o}_t}$ and liquidation cost $\frac{\partial \xi_{K_t}}{\partial \mathbb{o}_t}$,
- The relative utility-based price efficiencies of money, bonds, and capital $\mathcal{E}_a(\mathbb{o}_t)$,
- The steepening slope of marginal utility asymmetries across assets $\theta_a(\mathbb{o}_t)$,
- The narrowing margin between prevailing sentiment $\mathbb{o}_t$ and its critical bound $\mathbb{o}^C$.

Together, these metrics would have revealed that the system had entered a zone of self-fulfilling expectations, in which a sudden reversal in sentiment would provoke a macroeconomic reconfiguration far greater than its proximate trigger. In this sense, SAGE would have flagged the loss of structural resilience well before the formal onset of the crisis.

Historical data reveal that, after growing steadily for a prolonged period, sentiment eroded gradually across 2006 and 2007, particularly within financial markets. Mortgage delinquency rates were rising (Mian & Sufi, 2009). The ABX index, a derivative instrument tracking subprime mortgage performance, was plummeting (Gorton, 2009). Banks were tightening credit standards (FED, 2007). And interbank lending spreads—such as LIBOR-OIS—began to widen months before the crisis climax (Taylor & Williams, 2009). These developments reflected increasing uncertainty and declining confidence among key financial actors.

These indicators signaled that the system had entered a zone of self-fulfilling expectations, in which a further decline in sentiment—no matter how small its proximate trigger—would provoke a macroeconomic reconfiguration far greater than the initiating event. In SAGE terms, sentiment had approached its critical threshold $\mathbb{o}^C$, beyond which portfolio shifts would become rapid, nonlinear, and system-wide: from capital to liquidity, from investment to hoarding, from credit expansion to sudden stop.

By flagging these thresholds and amplifiers, SAGE would not have predicted the exact moment of crisis—but it would have diagnosed the progressive loss of resilience. It would have warned that the economy was structurally vulnerable to endogenous regime change, long before panic set in.

That said, a word of caution is warranted. The accurate identification of critical sentiment thresholds such as $\mathbb{o}^C$ poses significant empirical challenges. Measuring sentiment itself is nontrivial, and determining when it crosses structurally significant boundaries requires robust estimation techniques, high-frequency data, and deep contextual knowledge. This limitation does not undermine the SAGE framework, but highlights an important agenda for future research: developing empirical strategies to quantify sentiment elasticity, estimate tipping points, and track the dynamic evolution of $\theta_a(\mathbb{o}_t), \xi_a(\mathbb{o}_t)$, and $\sigma_a(\mathbb{o}_t)$ over time and across asset classes (see also Chap. 6).

Traditional early warning systems rely heavily on linear thresholds, macroprudential ratios, and backward-looking indicators. While they may flag imbalances—such as excessive leverage or asset bubbles—they typically fail to capture the deeper behavioral mechanics that render an economy structurally vulnerable. Critics often argue that no warning system could have predicted the scale of the 2007–09 collapse. SAGE does not challenge this view in terms of precise event prediction. Instead, it redefines what "warning" means: not as a signal of imminent rupture, but as the identification of conditions under which small perturbations can trigger regime shifts. Unlike traditional tools, SAGE explicitly models *endogenous fragility*—how sentiment interacts with asset valuation and expectations to produce self-reinforcing downturns. In this sense, the framework acts less like a seismograph for known shocks and more like a stress topology scanner: it highlights when the internal configuration of beliefs, liquidity preference, and portfolio exposure renders the system *dynamically unstable*, even in the absence of observable shocks.

With the above caveat, this case suggests how sentiment dynamics, as modeled in SAGE, allow for richer, real-time monitoring of macro-financial fragility. It reinforces the framework's central claim: that crisis is not always exogenous or sudden—it often brews in the shifting expectations and portfolio reallocations of forward-looking agents.

In conclusion, as a theoretical thought experiment, this exercise shows that had SAGE been operational and embedded in macro-financial surveillance frameworks, it could have highlighted the endogenous vulnerabilities that mainstream models systematically ignored. By making sentiment a first-order state variable, and by tracing its influence on asset preferences, utility valuation, and equilibrium multiplicity, SAGE offers a fundamentally different lens—one that does not reduce crises to exogenous anomalies but instead interprets them as emergent, predictable outcomes of sentiment-contingent dynamics. While this does not equate to forecasting precision, it marks a decisive step toward macroeconomic models that respect the reflexive nature of expectations and the complexity of modern financial systems.

References

Brunnermeier, M. K., & Pedersen, L. H. (2009). Market liquidity and funding liquidity. *The Review of Financial Studies, 22*(6), 2201–2238.

FED. (2007). *Senior loan officer opinion survey on Bank lending practices*. Board of Governors of the Federal Reserve System.

Gorton, G. (2009). Information, liquidity, and the (ongoing) panic of 2007. *American Economic Review: Papers & Proceedings, 99*(2), 567–572.

Gorton, G. B. (2010). *Slapped by the invisible hand: The panic of 2007*. Oxford University Press.

Mian, A., & Sufi, A. (2009). The consequences of mortgage credit expansion: Evidence from the U.S. mortgage default crisis. *Quarterly Journal of Economics, 124*(4), 1449–1496.

Taylor, J. B., & Williams, J. C. (2009). A black swan in the money market. *American Economic Journal: Macroeconomics, 1*(1), 58–83.

Chapter 6
Future Extensions and Applications of Sage

Abstract This chapter outlines future directions for extending SAGE into a general architecture for sentiment-responsive macroeconomic analysis. Key theoretical developments include introducing heterogeneous agents, overlapping generations, financial intermediaries, and feedback mechanisms between knowledge and sentiment. These would allow SAGE to capture asymmetric exposures to expectations, the endogenous dynamics of inequality, and cross-cohort or network-based contagion. Empirically, the chapter proposes strategies for estimating sentiment functions, calibrating asset utility parameters, and testing predictions on portfolio shifts, labor supply, innovation, and macro-financial instability. SAGE is also shown to apply across emerging domains where uncertainty, intertemporal coordination, and expectations formation are central—such as climate transition, artificial intelligence, digital monetary systems, and global financial interdependence. In these contexts, sentiment is not noise but structure: it shapes liquidity, investment, and risk in ways that are regime-dependent and policy-relevant. Methodologically, the chapter calls for embedding SAGE into stress testing, early warning, and simulation platforms. Ultimately, SAGE is positioned as an open and extensible system—combining cognitive realism, institutional grounding, and dynamic portfolio logic—to help reorient macroeconomics toward the informational, behavioral, and systemic realities of the twenty-first century.

SAGE opens the door to a wide range of applications across evolving economic domains. Its structure is uniquely suited to address the frontier challenges of twenty-first-century macroeconomics, where uncertainty, innovation, and sentiment dynamics dominate. This chapter outlines some future research trajectories that highlight SAGE's adaptive power.

Theoretical Refinements and Microfoundational Prospects Each of these future applications invites deeper theoretical developments. For instance, climate-related investment under SAGE may require modeling long-duration, low-liquidity assets with delayed utility payoffs. AI-enhanced agents may demand a probabilistic sentiment updating mechanism that adapts nonlinearly with signal noise and model uncertainty. Digital money, with programmable features and hybrid monetary

B. Bossone, *Bringing Sentiment into Economic Reason*, SpringerBriefs in Economics, https://doi.org/10.1007/978-3-032-08617-4_6

characteristics, challenges traditional notions of store-of-value and unit-of-account, and calls for dynamic utility terms that reflect network effects and trust. These adjustments do not contradict SAGE's structure; rather, they point to its extensibility across domains.

Financial Intermediation An important area for future work involves extending the current SAGE framework to explicitly model the role of financial intermediaries. While the existing formulation treats financial intermediation as a minimalistic mechanism that mirrors agents' portfolio allocation and investment decisions—deliberately simplified to focus on the effects of variable financial frictions—this abstraction limits the model's ability to capture the endogenous amplification dynamics triggered by intermediaries themselves. A more detailed representation of banks and other financial institutions would allow the framework to analyze how shocks originating within or outside the financial sector propagate and intensify through intermediation channels. This extension would be particularly valuable for examining systemic risk, procyclical leverage, and the interaction between financial conditions and real economic outcomes.

Dynamic Modeling and Multi-Agent Generalization Future research can also deepen SAGE's realism by extending it to dynamic, multi-agent, and even agent-based environments. In such models, heterogeneous sentiments, learning speeds, and financial frictions can produce richer endogenous macroeconomic patterns, such as herd behavior, market segmentation, or tipping-point phenomena. A multi-country SAGE model could simulate global contagion by allowing agents in one region to update sentiments based on foreign asset flows or narrative spillovers. Combining SAGE's rigor with complexity-aware modeling tools could position it as a next-generation framework for system-wide economic analysis.

Sentiment, Heterogeneity, and the Endogenous Dynamics of Inequality Once heterogeneity is introduced in SAGE, an additional natural extension of its framework—and hence an area for future research—involves incorporating agents with varying income levels, liquidity constraints, risk preferences, and investment horizons. This generalization—sketched conceptually throughout this chapter—would allow the model to speak more directly to distributional issues. Crucially, SAGE departs from standard heterogeneous-agent models by embedding belief-contingent utility at its core. The heterogeneity feature would enable the study of how sentiment-driven macroeconomic shifts affect agents asymmetrically, depending on their position in the wealth distribution and their exposure to illiquid assets. For instance, pessimistic sentiment may trigger defensive portfolio shifts and forced liquidations among liquidity-constrained households, while better-capitalized agents absorb distressed assets at favorable terms—producing belief-induced redistribution even in the absence of shocks or policy. Similarly, cycles of optimism and retrenchment can reshape the long-run distribution of wealth and investment opportunity across cohorts, especially in aging societies. By endogenizing both sentiment and its heterogeneous transmission, SAGE offers a promising framework to analyze the macroeconomic consequences of belief-driven inequality dynamics—an area still underexplored in the literature.

Developments of the OLG-SAGE Framework The integration of overlapping generations into the SAGE framework opens several promising avenues for future research. First, the current two-period structure could be expanded to a full multi-period lifecycle, incorporating endogenous retirement, health shocks, and mortality risk. Second, extending the sentiment dynamics to allow for cohort interaction and feedback loops—where older generations influence the expectations of younger ones through institutions, education, or media—would enhance realism. Third, a richer household optimization problem could endogenize fertility and bequest motives as functions of sentiment and perceived intergenerational contract stability. Finally, the belief kernel $\mathbb{K}_t$ could be further developed as a learning system responsive to public policy signals and social amplification dynamics, allowing sentiment equilibria to emerge, shift, or collapse in response to narrative shocks. These directions would deepen the model's ability to explain persistent low-growth equilibria, political-economic aging traps, and the fragility of macro-financial resilience in sentiment-fragmented societies.

Sentiment and Reason An important direction for future research lies in further exploring the reciprocal dynamics between the information and knowledge used by agents to form their expectations Ω and sentiment $\Omega^{'}$. While this book has treated information/knowledge and sentiment as interacting but separable state variables, a richer framework would allow for co-evolutionary feedbacks: the information and knowledge available to agents shape their sentiment, while sentiment affects which information agents attend to, how they filter or interpret it, and how they activate or weight elements of their knowledge base. Such mechanisms could introduce cognitive path dependence or even self-reinforcing belief regimes, where sentiment-influenced information processing perpetuates polarized or persistent expectations. Modeling this bidirectional influence would require formalizing endogenous shifts in epistemic salience—possibly drawing on insights from cognitive science, Bayesian learning under affective priors, or agent-based computational heuristics. Such developments hold promise for expanding the behavioral realism and explanatory range of SAGE.

Sentiment Threshold Estimation and Empirical Challenges A pressing avenue for future research concerns the identification of the sentiment threshold $\mathbb{o}^C$, beyond which regime shifts and macro-financial instability become likely. Because sentiment is an unobservable variable inferred from indirect indicators, empirical strategies must be developed to estimate its real-time dynamics with sufficient precision. Even in the presence of rich macro-financial data, there is considerable ambiguity in detecting when the system has crossed from resilience to fragility. To address this, researchers should prioritize estimating the sentiment elasticity of key asset variables—particularly price volatility $\sigma_a(\mathbb{o}_t)$, liquidation costs $\xi_a(\mathbb{o}_t)$, and utility weights $\theta_a(\mathbb{o}_t)$ across different asset portfolio classes. High-frequency portfolio allocation data, combined with sentiment indices and regime-switching econometric tools, could help uncover critical tipping points. Without such empirical calibration, the diagnostic power of SAGE remains suggestive rather than predictive. This task is especially urgent for macroprudential authorities seeking to build early warning systems based on sentiment-driven vulnerabilities.

Inflation as a Sentiment-Contingent Phenomenon Another important extension involves modeling inflation dynamics more explicitly under different sentiment regimes. The interaction between sentiment, liquidity preference, and money demand opens new ground for explaining both inflation inertia and nonlinear inflation outbursts. SAGE could be adapted to derive sentiment-adjusted Phillips-type relations, where inflation is driven not only by slack or wage growth but also by shifts in the perceived utility of money and assets, changes in institutional trust, or narrative shocks.

Climate Transition and Green Investment Dynamics The transition to a low-carbon economy is one of the defining macroeconomic challenges of our time. It entails vast reallocation of capital, long-horizon investment decisions, and deep uncertainty about regulatory regimes and technology paths. SAGE can model green investment as a distinct asset class with unique utility attributes—high long-term yield, but also high price volatility and low liquidity in the short run. Sentiment plays a crucial role here: rising public confidence in the green transition could shift portfolio allocations toward renewable capital, while policy missteps or credibility failures could trigger pessimism, delaying necessary investments. SAGE's endogenous treatment of expectations and liquidity makes it ideal for analyzing tipping points in climate finance, transition risks, and sentiment-driven coordination failures.

Artificial Intelligence and Expectations Formation Artificial intelligence (AI) is transforming information processing, forecasting, and decision-making across markets. SAGE can be extended to model agents with AI-augmented rationality—capable of using machine learning algorithms to form expectations based on complex data streams. This opens new analytical questions: How does AI affect market sentiment? Do AI agents converge faster to efficient equilibria, or can they amplify sentiment-driven cycles? Moreover, AI technologies may themselves become objects of portfolio investment, with their utility attributes evolving as adoption deepens. SAGE's structure is a promising foundation for modeling the macroeconomic consequences of algorithmic learning and collective expectation shifts in AI-permeated economies.

AI systems influence the credibility, speed, and volatility of information dissemination, thereby affecting sentiment formation and the expectations architecture within which agents operate. Future versions of SAGE could explicitly model the feedback loops between algorithmic learning, public narratives, and collective behavior—thus expanding its explanatory reach to the digital age.

Digital Assets and Monetary Architecture The rise of digital currencies and tokenized assets challenges the traditional definitions of money, liquidity, and financial intermediation. SAGE's utility-based treatment of money and financial assets allows it to naturally incorporate CBDCs, stablecoins, and crypto-assets as portfolio options. These instruments have distinct liquidity-speed profiles, volatility risks, and trust dependencies. SAGE can be used to assess how the coexistence of fiat and digital currencies affects aggregate demand, inflation dynamics, and monetary policy transmission. It can also model sentiment-driven volatility in crypto adoption or runs on digital assets triggered by confidence shocks. As the monetary architecture evolves, SAGE offers a robust platform for evaluating both systemic risk and financial innovation.

Global Contagion of Sentiment and Financial Spillovers In an interconnected world, sentiments do not stop at national borders. SAGE can be extended to a multi-country setting where sentiment shifts in one region spill over into others via trade, capital flows, and financial asset revaluation. A pessimistic shock in one large economy may trigger precautionary portfolio reallocations globally, leading to synchronized downturns. Conversely, confidence surges may spark excessive risk-taking across borders. SAGE's general equilibrium formulation enables modeling of such cross-border amplification, capturing how global narratives and expectations co-move with capital allocation and growth. This makes SAGE a powerful tool for analyzing the international transmission of crises, the limits of monetary and fiscal autonomy, and the design of coordination mechanisms in a sentiment-driven world.

Reframing Macroeconomic Policy A critical direction for future inquiry lies in rethinking the design, implementation, and evaluation of macroeconomic policy through SAGE. Because SAGE endogenizes expectations and sentiments, policy effectiveness depends not only on structural parameters but on the capacity of interventions to alter sentiment trajectories and portfolio incentives. This demands a fundamental re-evaluation of monetary, fiscal, and macroprudential strategies. What makes a policy credible in a SAGE world? How do communication strategies, institutional trust, and policy coordination shape sentiment dynamics? What are the risks of sentiment-induced policy ineffectiveness or overreach? Extending SAGE to formally model the sentiment-responsiveness of central bank and government behavior could generate new theoretical insights and practical tools for stabilizing economies prone to sentiment-driven instability. SAGE thus opens a fertile research agenda at the intersection of policy credibility, behavioral expectations, and macro-financial resilience. Promising application domains include macroprudential surveillance, stress testing, and crisis prediction. In particular, integrating SAGE into central bank models could enhance early warning systems by identifying thresholds that signal vulnerability to self-fulfilling crises. Another area is sovereign debt sustainability: sentiment-contingent discount factors may yield more accurate projections than purely fundamentals-based models. To operationalize these ideas, one possible line of work involves computational simulations of sentiment dynamics under heterogeneous-agent settings. Another avenue is empirical calibration of the utility efficiency parameters using macro-financial time-series data. Sentiment indices (e.g., consumer confidence, investor sentiment surveys) and high-frequency portfolio allocation data can help estimate the thresholds and feedback loops highlighted in Chap. 4. Such work would allow testing SAGE's predictions regarding bifurcations, regime shifts, and nonlinear recovery dynamics.

Conclusion

This book has proposed the **S**entiment-**A**ugmented **G**eneral **E**quilibrium (**SAGE**) framework as a unified theory of intertemporal choice, finance, and economic growth, which integrates human sentiment and rational expectations into the core of macroeconomic modeling. SAGE answers a central and enduring question in economics: how do agents make decisions under uncertainty in a world of imperfect and incomplete information, evolving expectations, and financial frictions—and how do these micro-level decisions aggregate into the complex macroeconomic phenomena we observe?

SAGE seeks to unify fragmented strands of macroeconomic theory on three foundational concepts: reason, sentiment, and utility. The first two—reason and sentiment—interact dynamically and together constitute the cognitive-affective essence of human agency. The third, utility, serves as the universal metric through which all economic objects and activities are evaluated intra- and inter-temporally and chosen by agents under uncertainty.

SAGE recognizes that agents derive intra- and inter-temporal utility not only from consumption and leisure but also from the very (monetary, financial, and nonfinancial) assets they hold. These assets are not inert stores of value. They are active vehicles to real resources, whose desirability depends on their speed (liquidity) and power (return-generating capacity), and whose relative appeal varies with agents' expectations and sentiments. This structural treatment of asset utility marks a decisive shift from earlier models where financial instruments entered the economy only through constraints or exogenous frictions.

A distinguishing contribution of SAGE is the formal incorporation of sentiment into the heart of economic decision-making. In contrast to models that treat expectations as either fully rational or arbitrarily behavioral, SAGE models expectations as rational but they are formed by processing available information through a sentiment filter that captures optimism or pessimism about the future. This filter is endogenous. It evolves with the economic environment, responds to macro-financial signals, and feeds back into the decisions that shape the trajectory of the economy itself. In doing

B. Bossone, *Bringing Sentiment into Economic Reason*, SpringerBriefs in Economics, https://doi.org/10.1007/978-3-032-08617-4

so, SAGE reflects the reality that human agents, while rational, are also influenced by emotion, confidence, trust, and narrative context.

This dual and yet integrated grounding—in rationality and sentiment—allows SAGE to replicate and explain features of macroeconomic dynamics that remain elusive in conventional models. It shows how agents' perceptions of asset risk, liquidity, and utility can give rise to multiple equilibria, endogenous cycles, and path-dependent stagnation or growth. Boom–bust dynamics, liquidity traps, and secular stagnation emerge not as anomalies or externally imposed shocks, but as natural outcomes of optimizing behavior in environments shaped by evolving sentiments and market conditions. SAGE's account of stagnation, in particular, represents a conceptual breakthrough: it identifies how a shift in sentiment below a critical threshold can trigger a self-reinforcing regime of low investment, weak innovation, and liquidity hoarding—even in the absence of fundamental shocks or policy errors.

The OLG extension of SAGE broadens the scope of the framework by introducing demographic structure and intergenerational belief transmission. The incorporation of a sentiment-contingent rational-expectations kernel provides a flexible and tractable way to model generational memory and narrative-driven expectations, offering a powerful lens through which to analyze low-growth traps, demographic cycles, and the shifting effectiveness of macro policy.

A core contribution of SAGE lies in its reconstruction of growth theory around choice and financial decisions. Unlike classical or Schumpeterian frameworks, growth in SAGE is not driven purely by factor accumulation or exogenous innovation, but by the evolving interplay between marginal utility of assets, rational expectations, and sentiment. Shifts in sentiment influence investment in physical and intangible capital, altering the economy's innovative capacity and its long-run productive frontier. SAGE opens a new path for growth theory—one where the economy's trajectory is not merely a function of technology and policy, but of the collective psychology that shapes capital formation itself.

Another critical insight from SAGE is the role of saving in growth. Contrary to traditional models, it is not the aggregate volume of saving that determines long-term performance, but its **composition**—how intertemporal resources are allocated across assets with varying liquidity, volatility, and productive potential. Growth depends on the economy's capacity to mobilize savings toward illiquid but high-yield investments, under conditions of trust, patience, and manageable risk. When sentiment favors liquid or speculative assets—due to fear, uncertainty, or institutional fragility—aggregate saving may remain high, yet investment and growth stagnate. In this light, **growth becomes a portfolio-driven outcome**, shaped as much by confidence and intermediation quality as by resource accumulation itself.

Equally significant is SAGE's reinterpretation of canonical empirical puzzles. The equity premium puzzle, for instance, is no longer a paradox requiring extreme risk aversion or exotic preferences. It becomes a predictable result of differences in asset utility: capital must offer higher returns because it is perceived as less liquid and more volatile—especially in pessimistic environments. Similarly, exchange rate overshooting can be understood not as a failure of price rigidity assumptions, but as a rational response to portfolio reallocations triggered by sentiment shocks. These reinterpretations are not add-ons; they are derived directly from the framework's core logic. In this way, SAGE demonstrates the explanatory power of integrating utility-based portfolio choice with expectations.

SAGE reinterprets inflation not simply as a price response to slack or money growth, but as an equilibrium outcome shaped by shifting portfolio preferences, trust in the value of money, and the liquidity premium households assign under varying sentiments. Such an approach explains both disinflationary traps and inflationary bursts without relying on exogenous shocks or arbitrary expectations assumptions.

Beyond theory, SAGE offers a foundation for rethinking macroeconomic policy. It implies that monetary, fiscal, and financial policies operate not just through mechanical levers, but through their capacity to influence expectations, portfolio preferences, and perceived systemic stability. In the SAGE world, credibility is endogenous and dynamic. Policy effectiveness depends on its ability to coordinate sentiments, reinforce trust, and shift the marginal utility of risk-taking versus liquidity preference. This perspective recasts the role of institutions—not as background parameters, but as essential components of economic dynamics. It also raises the bar for policy design: stabilizing the economy requires not only technical skill but also narrative clarity, institutional strength, and communicative effectiveness.

Methodologically, SAGE bridges a major gap in macroeconomic modeling. It restores behavioral realism—by incorporating sentiment, liquidity, and sentiment dynamics—without abandoning tractability or coherence. The framework remains analytically rigorous and internally consistent, yet rich enough to generate nonlinear paths, multiple equilibria, and endogenous instability. It avoids the hyper-rational abstraction of representative-agent DSGE models and the opaque complexity of purely agent-based simulations, offering instead a structured, general utility-theoretic architecture capable of capturing real-world dynamics with theoretical discipline.

Also, while the current version of SAGE adopts a representative-agent structure for tractability, with its limitations, it is well-suited to studying environments where sentiment-contingent expectations are broadly shared—whether due to short-term informational alignment or longer-term demographic influences. Nonetheless, extending the model to incorporate heterogeneous agents remains an important avenue for future development. Indeed, as discussed in Chap. 6, SAGE's extension to heterogeneous agents holds promise also for modeling the uneven transmission of sentiment shocks and their long-run distributional consequences—a crucial frontier for both theory and policy.

Epistemologically, SAGE proposes a reframing of what macroeconomics is and should be. It moves the field from a narrow science of optimization under constraint to a broader inquiry into how expectations, narratives, and institutional structures interact to shape collective economic behavior. In this sense, SAGE is more than a model: it is a conceptual bridge—between choice and context, between structure and story, between rationality and sentiment. It points toward a macroeconomics that is not only unified but also human, historically grounded, and systemically aware.

Finally, it is important to clarify what SAGE deliberately chooses not to be. Although it shares analytical concerns with complexity economics—such as endogenous feedbacks, multiple equilibria, and nonlinear dynamics—it does not build on complexity theory in the formal sense. SAGE does not rely on agent-based simulations, network effects, or large-scale heterogeneity. Instead, it follows a parsimonious modeling strategy: a tractable, utility-based framework that integrates sentiment and financial frictions into general equilibrium reasoning. In this sense, SAGE offers a complementary alternative to complexity-based approaches—explaining persistent macro-financial anomalies with minimal structural assumptions, and doing so in a way that is both transparent and extensible.

The analytical thought experiment on the 2007–09 crisis underscores SAGE's ability to reinterpret macro-financial instability as a product of endogenous sentiment dynamics. The framework shows how shifts in perceived systemic trust, liquidity risk, and utility-based asset desirability could have signaled an impending regime switch well before headline indicators collapsed. It illuminates how optimistic equilibria can be destabilized by self-reinforcing portfolio shifts and volatility spirals, especially when sentiment falls below a critical threshold. This interpretation reinforces the idea that crises need not be triggered by exogenous shocks—they can emerge from within, when the underlying structure of beliefs and preferences loses its coherence. In this light, SAGE provides not only a diagnostic lens but also a prospective tool for policy foresight and institutional design.

Looking ahead, SAGE opens fertile ground for applied and theoretical research. It can be extended to model climate-related investment, AI-enhanced forecasting, digital asset competition, global financial spillovers, and policy transmission. It invites richer microfoundations through heterogeneous-agent modeling and greater complexity awareness through simulation-based tools.

Future research should prioritize the empirical validation of SAGE's predictions. Key targets include estimating sentiment thresholds, identifying early warning signs of stagnation traps, and testing the asymmetric response of capital demand to sentiment shifts. Collaborations across central banks, academic institutions, and data platforms could operationalize SAGE for real-time policy diagnostics and crisis prevention. Growth theory, in particular, presents a promising frontier: quantifying how belief dynamics shape capital formation, institutional quality, and productivity gains will be essential to harnessing SAGE's full potential.

In sum, SAGE provides a foundational step toward a more realistic, coherent, and policy-relevant macroeconomic science—one capable of addressing the complexities and fragilities of our time, and of illuminating the uncertain paths ahead.

Appendices

Appendix A. Foundational Concepts: Sentiment, Reason, and Utility

At the heart of SAGE lie three foundational concepts: sentiment, reason, and utility. These are not auxiliary features appended to a traditional rational choice model; rather, they form the ontological core of how economic behavior is modeled in SAGE. They define how agents perceive their environment, form expectations, and allocate resources under uncertainty. The first two concepts—reason and sentiment—interact dynamically and together constitute the cognitive-affective essence of human agency. The third concept, utility, serves as the encompassing metric through which all economic objects and activities—production, exchange, and consumption—are evaluated and chosen. By placing these three constructs at the foundation of the model, SAGE departs from both conventional rational expectations frameworks and behaviorally adjusted models. It advances instead a psychologically and institutionally grounded theory of choice, portfolio allocation, and macroeconomic dynamics.

This appendix defines the meanings and interactions of these three core concepts. It also examines the dynamic interdependence of the three elements: sentiment guides perception and valuation, reason structures information processing and belief updating, and utility captures how both affect and cognition are translated into preferences and behavior. This architecture allows SAGE to explain persistent real-world phenomena—such as secular stagnation, asset mispricing, capital flights, growth, labor market dynamics, and inflation shocks—as rational, sentiment-contingent outcomes within an integrated decision-making framework.

Sentiment as Structured Affect

In SAGE, sentiment is formalized as a state variable that captures agents' affective orientation toward future economic outcomes. It is neither a transient mood nor an irrational impulse. Rather, sentiment reflects an affectively structured, cognitively

B. Bossone, *Bringing Sentiment into Economic Reason*, SpringerBriefs in Economics, https://doi.org/10.1007/978-3-032-08617-4

mediated disposition—one that is shaped by information, narratives, institutional trust, and social interactions.

Unlike traditional models where expectations are formed independently of emotion, or behavioral models that treat sentiment as an exogenous shock, SAGE makes sentiment endogenous and recursive. The sentiment variable $\Omega' \in (0, 1)$ orients agents' forecasts, influences their perception of risks, and shifts the subjective probabilities they assign to future outcomes (see Chap. 3). High values of Ω' (optimism) lead agents to anticipate smoother consumption paths and lower liquidity needs, thereby reducing the marginal utility of money and increasing investment in higher-yielding assets. Low values of Ω' (pessimism) induce precautionary behavior, liquidity hoarding, and delayed investment.

As noted in Chap. 2, this conception of sentiment is rooted in findings from neuroscience and cognitive psychology, which demonstrate that affective states influence not just what agents feel but how they interpret, prioritize, and act upon information. Sentiment is thus not a deviation from rationality, but an essential component of situated rational behavior under uncertainty.

SAGE goes further by embedding sentiment in a recursive structure: sentiment shapes expectations, and expectations (as they are validated or disconfirmed by observed events) feed back into sentiment. This feedback loop makes a genuine state variable whose dynamics contribute to endogenous regime shifts and multiple equilibria.

Reason as Contextual Rationality

Reason in the SAGE framework refers to the agent's structured cognitive capacity to process information, update beliefs, and make forward-looking decisions. Importantly, reason is not treated as omniscient or purely deductive. Instead, it is modeled as a **contextual inferential mechanism**—bounded, fallible, and shaped by both the quality of available information and the agent's prevailing sentiment.

Formally, each agent is characterized by a state-of-knowledge parameter $\Omega \in (0, 1)$, which indexes the precision and reliability of the probability distributions they use to forecast future variables (see Chap. 4). Higher implies narrower, better-anchored expectations; lower implies wider, more diffuse beliefs. Sentiment Ω' interacts with Konwldge-state Ω by orienting which distributions are emphasized—biasing expectations either upward or downward relative to what a purely data-driven inference would suggest.

In SAGE, reason and sentiment co-evolve: agents do not abandon rationality, but their rationality is contextual—embedded in a cognitive-affective environment that shapes how they interpret risk, credibility, and opportunity.

The Sentiment–Reason–Utility Nexus

The true innovation of the SAGE framework lies in how it integrates sentiment, reason, and utility into a recursive, interdependent system. Each of the three elements shapes and is shaped by the others:

- **Sentiment** orients agents' interpretation of uncertainty and modifies how they form expectations.

- **Reason** structures information processing and belief updating, conditioned by sentiment.
- **Utility** captures how these beliefs are translated into preferences, guiding the allocation of wealth and labor.

This recursive triad generates path-dependent dynamics: changes in sentiment can shift expectations, which in turn alter portfolio allocations, investment flows, and ultimately macroeconomic outcomes. These outcomes feed back into observed indicators, updating sentiment and reason, further affecting allocative choices, and producing new macroeconomic outcomes. The result is an economy in which multiple equilibria, sentiment-driven volatility, and self-reinforcing stagnation or exuberance are not anomalies—they are intrinsic possibilities.

Utility as a Generalized Metric of Preference

In SAGE, utility is expanded and generalized to encompass all allocable resources—consumption goods, labor, leisure, money, bonds, other financial instruments, capital, and other real assets. The utility function is not limited to consumption flows; it includes the liquidity, price volatility, liquidation cost, and future return characteristics of financial and productive assets. Assets deliver utility not simply because they finance consumption, but because they serve as vehicles that enable their holders to carry forward access to real resources across time and states of nature, each with varying "speed" (liquidity) and "power" (store-of-value capacity).

A utility function is defined to represent that agents derive from holding real, monetary and financial resources over time facing an uncertain future (see Chap. 3). The partial utilities from holding assets are adjusted by sentiment-contingent discount factors that reflect expected liquidation costs, price volatility, and opportunity costs. These adjustments capture how market structure, institutional trust, and mood shape the real-time utility derived from holding various assets.

SAGE differs by deriving the utility of money and assets endogenously from their liquidity and volatility attributes, which are in turn shaped by sentiment and institutional quality. This endogenization allows SAGE to model rational portfolio shifts under changing belief regimes, without invoking external shocks or ad hoc preference shifts.

Implications for Economic Modeling

Integrating sentiment, reason, and utility into the core structure of economic modeling redefines the analytical landscape. It enables SAGE to:

- Offer **microfounded explanations** for liquidity preference, portfolio shifts, and macro-volatility.
- Model **expectations as belief systems** shaped by both cognitive capacity and affective orientation.
- Account for **institutional structure and credibility** not as external parameters, but as endogenous determinants of utility and behavior.

This foundational architecture allows SAGE to bridge economics with psychology, neuroscience, and institutional theory, while preserving the rigor of general equilibrium analysis. It repositions macroeconomics as a science of **situated human agency**—where decisions are made under uncertainty by emotionally and cognitively engaged agents embedded in evolving social and institutional environments.

This redefinition is not merely conceptual—it is operational. SAGE's formal model builds directly on this foundation, using sentiment, reason, and utility as the generative mechanisms for systemic dynamics and policy-relevant outcomes.

Appendix B. Constructing the Sentiment Variable Ω'

A simple way to build variable Ω', which reflects the agents' *perceived* state of the world, introduced in block 3 of the model, is to use backward and forward indicators that capture, respectively, past and future economic dynamics. Simple examples of such indicators include the following:

(a) *General economic stability:* this is evaluated in terms of social loss function $L = L(\overline{x})$, where $\overline{x}$ is the set of arguments representing the key macroeconomic policy objectives pursued by the policymakers, and each argument is expressed as a deviation between actual and target values. Agents know that policymakers pursue socially optimal target $T^* = minL(\overline{x})$. They, thus, observe the actual values of T and compare them to T^*, and grant equal weight to negative and positive deviations of equal value. Looking backward, say τ periods from current date t_0, the agents evaluate economic stability using the quadratic function:

$$S = -\sum_{t=t_0-\tau}^{t_0-1}\left(\frac{1}{t}\right)(T_t - T^*)^2 = S(\Lambda, t), \text{ where } (T_t - T^*) \equiv \Lambda_t \text{ with } S'_\Lambda < 0, S'_t > 0, \tag{B.1}$$

where recent deviations Λ weigh more heavily than distant ones. Note that S increases with lower Λ and with higher scalar factor t, which determines the duration of (in)stability: all else equal, a value of S calculated over a longer time interval is more informative than if calculated over a shorter interval. In words: protracted stability (instability) feeds optimism (pessimism).

(b) *Past economic performances:* these are measured as observed changes in the past realizations of some relevant variables (e.g., GDP growth, inflation, unemployment, etc.) over a given period:

$$PEP_t = \sum_{t=t_0-\tau}^{t_0-1}\left(\frac{1}{t}\right)(X_t - X_{t-1}), \tag{B.2}$$

where observations distant in time weigh less than those closer to the present and persistent same-directional changes increase the value of the indicator.

(c) *Expected future performances:* these are measured as future discounted expected values of relevant variable market performances over a foreseeable period:

$$FEP_t = \sum\nolimits_{t=t_0-\tau}^{t_0-1} \left(\frac{1}{t}\right) E_{t_0}(X_t - X_{t-1}). \tag{B.3}$$

From Eqs. (B.1)–(B.3), define

$$\Omega = \Omega(S, PEP, FEP), \text{with } \Omega'_S, \Omega'_{PEP}, \Omega'_{FEP} > 0,$$

that is, increasing perceptions of economic stability, improving past market performances, and improving expected future market performance generate greater optimism and vice versa.

As noted in the text, the relevance of the above indicators does not lie in their specific form, but in that they reflect the notion that agent emotions are not unexplained "sunspots" and derive, instead, from the ongoing interactions of human states of mind with information, knowledge, and rationality and their influence on agent responses to real circumstances. Integrating or replacing these indicators with others, including more sophisticated ones and covering other aspects of the economy, would not alter this basic understanding.

Appendix C. Derivation of the Reduced-Form Equation for Asset Utility

This appendix shows how reduced-form Eq. (3.6) in the text was derived from the general asset utility function, for use under greater tractability. The general equation is:

$$u(a_t) = u(a_t; \omega_t) = E_t\left\{\beta R^a_{t+1}\left\{u\left(\frac{P^a_{t+1}a_t}{P_{C,\tau}}\right)\vartheta_{t+1}(\omega_t)\right.\right.$$
$$\left.\left. + \sum_{\tau=t+1}^{T=\infty} \beta^\tau \prod_{\tau=t+1}^{T=\infty} u\left(\frac{P^a_\tau a_t}{P_{C,\tau}}\right) R^a_\tau [1 - \vartheta_\tau(\omega_t)][1 - \xi_{a_\tau}(\omega_t)]\left[1 - \sigma^a_\tau(\omega_t)\right]\vartheta_{t+1}(\omega_t)\right\}\right\}. \tag{C.1}$$

Assume the period utility function is logarithmic over consumption-like quantities:

$$u(x) = \ln(x), \text{with } x = \frac{P^a_\tau a_t}{P_\tau}$$

Rewrite now Eq. (C.1) in terms of expected log consumption-equivalent values of assets. This collapses to:

$$u(a_t; \mathbb{o}_t) = \mathbb{E}_t\left\{\sum_{\tau=t+1}^{\infty} \beta^\tau \vartheta_\tau(\mathbb{o}_t)\, log\, \frac{P_\tau^a a_t}{P_{C,\tau}} R_{a_t}\right\}.$$

Notice that the weights $\beta^\tau, \vartheta_\tau, and\ R_{a_t}$ form a decaying kernel over time.

Assuming a geometrically distributed liquidation horizon with expected length h and approximately constant returns, prices and probabilities, the infinite discounted sum collapses to an effective utility term. With transaction cost ξ_{a_τ} and return variance $\sigma_{a,\ \tau}$ entering as discounting factors:

$$u(a_t; \mathbb{o}_t) \approx \theta_a(\mathbb{o}_t)\vartheta_a\, log\left(\frac{P_\tau^a}{P_{C,\tau}} \frac{a_t}{C_t} \frac{1}{1 + \xi_{K_t}(\mathbb{o}_t) + \sigma_{K_t}(\mathbb{o}_t).}\right), \tag{C.2}$$

where $\theta_a(\mathbb{o}_t)$ is the utility weight applied to asset a (see also Appendix D); $\vartheta_a = \sum_{\tau=t+1}^{\infty} \beta^\tau \vartheta_\tau(\mathbb{o}_t) R_{a_t}$; and $\frac{1}{1+\xi_{K_t}(\mathbb{o}_t)+\sigma_{K_t}(\mathbb{o}_t).}$ is the sentiment-contingent discount factor. Equation (C.2) is the reduced-form equation used in the text.

Appendix D. The Asset Preference Weights θ_a

At first glance, the parameters $\theta_a \in \{M, B, K\}$—which weight the utility derived from holding assets in the household's utility function—might seem like standard preference coefficients. Yet in SAGE, they play a far more intricate and revealing role. Far from being arbitrary taste parameters, the θ_a's represent reduced-form summaries of intra- and inter-temporal utility that are shaped by rational expectations, financial frictions, and—most crucially—sentiment.

These weights act as equilibrium reflections of how much utility the representative agent expects to derive from each asset, relative to consumption, under prevailing beliefs and constraints. They translate the deep structure of forward-looking optimization into a tractable format that can be analyzed and interpreted within a general equilibrium model. In this sense, the θ_a's are bridging variables: they connect the psychological, social, financial, and structural layers of economic behavior into a single coherent representation.

This appendix develops the analytical foundation of θ_a, interprets their role within the SAGE model, and highlights their broader significance for understanding macro-financial dynamics in economies.

Reduced-Form Utility Weights

The starting point is the general expression for the utility that a household derives from holding an asset a, introduced in Sect. 3.1:

$$u(a_t) = u(a_t; \circledcirc_t) = E_t\left\{\beta R_{a,t+1}\left\{u\left(\frac{P^a_{t+1}a_t}{P_{C,\tau}}\right)\vartheta_{t+1}(\circledcirc_t)\right.\right.$$

$$\left.\left. + \sum_{\tau=t+1}^{T=\infty}\beta^\tau \prod_{\tau=t+1}^{T=\infty} u\left(\frac{P^a_\tau a_t}{P_{C,\tau}}\right)R_{a,t}\left[1-\vartheta_\tau(\circledcirc_t)\right]\left[1-\xi_{a_\tau}(\circledcirc_t)\right]\left[1-\sigma^a_\tau(\circledcirc_t)\right]\vartheta_{t+1}(\circledcirc_t)\right\}\right\}.$$

Here, the household faces uncertainty over when the asset may need to be liquidated (governed by the probability $\vartheta_{t\,+\,1}$), how costly liquidation would be (captured by ξ_a), and how risky the price path of the asset may turn out to be (reflected in σ_a). Expectations are formed rationally but are shaped by sentiment, so that the probabilities themselves vary with the sentiment $\circledcirc_t$. In a world of complete certainty and frictionless markets, this utility stream might collapse to a standard present-discounted value. But under the SAGE framework, agents live in a world of radical uncertainty, evolving beliefs, and financial constraints. This complexity must be captured in a way that is analytically tractable but still faithful to the behavioral and institutional underpinnings of the model. Hence the move to the reduced-form representation derived in Appendix C:

$$u(a_t; \circledcirc_t) \approx \theta_a(\circledcirc_t)\vartheta_a \, log\left(\frac{P^a_\tau}{P_{C,\tau}}\,\frac{a_t}{C_t}\,\frac{1}{1+\xi_{K_t}(\circledcirc_t)+\sigma_{K_t}(\circledcirc_t).}\right).$$

In this form, the entire forward-looking structure is compressed into a single term: $\theta_a(\circledcirc_t)$. This term aggregates, in equilibrium, the expected marginal utility of wealth allocated to asset a, adjusted for liquidation frictions and volatility, and conditional on sentiment. It is the behavioral shadow cast by the deeper, utility stream.

Meaning of $\boldsymbol{\theta_a}$

To appreciate the full significance of θ_a, consider its role in the household's optimization problem. In the reduced-form utility function (Eq. 3.6), $\theta_a(\circledcirc_t)$ reflects the marginal utility of wealth allocated to asset a relative to consumption:

$$\theta_a(\circledcirc_t) = \frac{\partial U_t}{\partial a_t} / \frac{\partial U_t}{\partial C_t} \mid \circledcirc_t.$$

This expression tells how much utility the agent expects to gain from allocating an extra unit of real wealth to asset a, rather than consuming it today. Yet, unlike standard marginal utilities, which are fixed by preferences alone, θ_a is fundamentally endogenous. It shifts with the agent's expectations about future income and consumption needs, the perceived liquidity and price volatility of the asset, and the prevailing state of sentiment.

When optimism prevails, the agent expects smooth consumption and few liquidity shocks. Illiquid, high-yielding assets like capital K become more attractive. This pushes up θ_K and reduces θ_M and θ_B. In contrast, when pessimism dominates, future consumption is seen as more uncertain and immediate liquidity becomes valuable. Money then regains its utility premium, raising θ_M and θ_B relative to θ_K. In this way, θ_a encapsulates the entire behavioral and structural logic of SAGE.

Comparative Statics

Understanding how θ_a responds to changes in sentiment, risk, and frictions helps us anticipate how portfolio choices and macroeconomic outcomes evolve. Some key relationships include:

Sentiment ω_t

- $\frac{\partial \theta M_t}{\partial \omega_t} < 0$: Optimism reduces the value of money holdings.
- $\frac{\partial \theta K_t}{\partial \omega_t} > 0$: Optimism increases the attractiveness of capital.
- θ_B may exhibit a non-monotonic relationship: safe in downturns, but less rewarding in booms.

Volatility σ_a

- $\frac{\partial \theta_{a,t}}{\partial \sigma_{a,t}} < 0$: Assets that are more volatile provide less utility per unit of real wealth.

Liquidation Cost ξ_a

- $\frac{\partial \theta_{a,t}}{\partial \xi_{a,t}} < 0$: Greater friction reduces the utility derived from holding the asset.

These sensitivities reflect the agent's attempt to optimize under uncertainty: when the environment becomes riskier or more illiquid, the utility-maximizing portfolio tilts toward assets that provide safety, even if they offer lower yields.

Relevance of θ_a

While θ_a emerges from a theoretical model, it has clear empirical resonance. In practice, the behavior of these weights can be inferred from changes in portfolio allocations across asset classes, movements in consumption-wealth ratios, and shifts in sentiment indices such as consumer confidence or financial stress indicators. Cross-country and time-series comparisons can also shed light on how institutional quality, financial development, or policy credibility influence the dynamics of θ_a. For instance, in fragile economies, θ_M may remain structurally high, reflecting persistent liquidity preference, while in mature economies with deep markets and stable policy regimes, θ_K may dominate under normal conditions, but still collapse in response to crises of confidence. This flexibility makes θ_a a powerful diagnostic tool for understanding both microeconomic behavior and macroeconomic pathologies.

Broader Implications

The deeper purpose of formalizing θ_a is not merely technical. It is also philosophical and methodological. By embedding expectations and sentiment directly into utility, SAGE reconfigures how we understand the very nature of economic reasoning. In traditional models, preferences are fixed and sentiment is either ignored or exogenously added. In SAGE, the agents' valuation of assets—their very utility—is shaped by their state of belief about the world. This bears opens several implications:

- Policy interventions may fail not because they lack magnitude, but because they do not move sentiment—and hence do not shift θ_a.
- Equilibria may bifurcate: the same structural fundamentals can support very different allocations, prices, and dynamics depending on the constellation of θ_a values.
- Financial stability becomes a function of how agents perceive and value their asset positions under uncertainty.

Macroeconomic stability depends on whether the weights θ_a tilt toward resilience or fragility.

Appendix E. The Household's Job Value

In calculating its intertemporal budget constraint, the household evaluates its future income perspectives by considering its job value, that is, the present-discounted value of the future difference between a worker's productivity and the worker's current pay (Hall, 2003),[1]

$$JV_t = \mathbb{E}_t[\sum_{\tau=t+1}^{\infty}(\prod_{i=t}^{\tau}\beta_i)(p_\tau x_\tau - w_\tau)|\omega_t], \tag{E.1}$$

where x and w are, respectively, the household's output and remuneration, and expectations $\mathbb{E}_t$ reflect changing market moods ω at time t (to be discussed later): the job value declines with pessimistic prospects about future levels of remuneration and risk of unemployment (and vice versa with optimistic prospects). It is assumed that the household forms expectations of future incomes y as:

$$\mathbb{E}_t[y_\tau|\omega_t] = \mathbb{E}_t\left[y_\tau^{\{[JV_\tau(\omega_t)/\overline{\Pi}]\}}\right], \tag{E.2}$$

where $\overline{\Pi}$ is the normal rate of profit earned by the firm employing the household labor services; $\frac{JV_t}{\overline{\Pi}} = 1$ holds under normal economic conditions; and $\frac{JV_t}{\overline{\Pi}} > 1$ (< 1) under optimistic (pessimistic) expectations. The household expects a higher or lower future income level (or an interruption of income) depending on how the prevailing

[1] Hall, cit., defines "job value" as the value of a filled job to the employer as the present value of the flow of profits generated by employing a worker, net of wages and other costs. This value plays a critical role in determining firms' willingness to post vacancies and create new jobs.

sentiment affects its own expectations (and those of the enterprises) and reflects on the job value estimates. Eq. (E.1) can be considered as an expression for household permanent income built on expectations and sentiment and provides an important channel to which uncertainty (and, specifically, idiosyncratic uninsurable risks) can be introduced in the model. Eqs. (E.1)–(E.2) introduce two very important features of the model:

- First, household future income does not just stochastically fluctuate around its full-employment level: households do factor into their plans the possibility of protracted periods of underemployment or unemployment income. This feature is consistent with the findings by Guvenen (2017) on income risk.
- Second, although (as discussed below) price responses to demand shocks are not considered in this appendix, Eqs. (E.1)–(E.2) suggest that, especially in deflationary environments, price adjustments might not provide simple equilibrating mechanisms since expected price (and wage) dynamics enter the job value estimates and reflect on the demand responses.

Appendix F. Existence of Critical Sentiment Threshold ϖ^C

The existence of a critical sentiment threshold ϖ^C is not automatic, it must emerge endogenously from the interaction of utility, expectations, and portfolio trade-offs in SAGE. However, under plausible conditions, such a threshold can be shown to exist and to govern a discontinuous shift in equilibrium behavior. Here's a structured explanation that can be incorporated into your manuscript to formalize why and under what conditions ϖ^* exists.

Recall that capital's utility contribution is:

$$U_K \mid \varpi = \frac{\omega_K}{1 + (\xi_K + \sigma_K) \mid \varpi} = \frac{\omega_K}{\Delta\mathcal{E}_{K,t} \mid \varpi_t},$$

with $\frac{\partial \xi_K}{\partial \varpi} < 0$, $\frac{\partial^2 \xi_K}{\partial \varpi^2} > 0$, $\frac{\partial \sigma_K}{\partial \varpi} < 0$, $\frac{\partial^2 \sigma_K}{\partial \varpi^2} > 0$. Thus, $\Delta\mathcal{E}_{K,t} \mid \varpi_t$ is a decreasing and convex function of ϖ and $U_K \mid \varpi$ is increasing and concave in ϖ. This introduces nonlinear sentiment sensitivity into the utility of capital relative to liquid assets.

Now consider the first-order condition whereby $U_K \mid \varpi = U_M \mid \varpi$, balancing marginal utility-based, returns on capital and money, respectively. As sentiment falls, $U_K \mid \varpi$ collapses, while $U_M \mid \varpi$ rises.

At some critical $\varpi = \varpi^C$, this trade-off crosses a discontinuity: the household abruptly reallocates away from capital. This is where the interior solution for capital demand becomes unstable, and the economy shifts to corner-solution behavior (capital hoarding collapses, liquidity hoarding dominates).

Notice that the general condition for the existence of ϖ^C can be derived as follows. Let $f(\varpi) = U_K \mid \varpi - U_M \mid \varpi$, then ϖ^C exists if $f(\varpi)$ crosses zero from above at some interior $\varpi \in (0, 1)$, i.e.,

$$\begin{cases} f(\mathbf{o}) > 0 \text{ for high } \mathbf{o}, \\ f(\mathbf{o}) < 0 \text{ for low } \mathbf{o}, \\ \quad f'^{(\mathbf{o})} < 0 \text{ near crossing point.} \end{cases}$$

This is a standard intermediate value theorem condition. If $U_K \mid \mathbf{o}$ is decresing and convex and $U_M \mid \mathbf{o}$ is increasing and concave in $\mathbf{o}$, then a unique threshold $\mathbf{o}^C$ exists at which the agent switches from capital-holding to liquidity-hoarding. Therefore, $\mathbf{o}^C$ can be defined as the tipping point where:

$$U_K \mid \mathbf{o}^C = U_M \mid \mathbf{o}^C \text{ and } \frac{\partial(U_K - U_M)}{\partial \mathbf{o}} < 0,$$

that is, the point beyond which the indifference between capital and money becomes unstable.

In economic terms, the threshold $\mathbf{o}^C$ captures a sentiment-induced switch in optimal behavior. It reflects the point below (above) which the expected costs of holding capital exceed (fall short of) its benefits, given perceived market conditions (illiquidity, volatility, risk). It is not a fixed parameter, but rather a state-contingent object that emerges from the model's utility structure and expectations.

Appendix G. Stability Conditions for the Capital–Sentiment Dynamics

Consider the two-dimensional first-order system:

$$\begin{cases} K_{t+1} = k(K_t, \mathbf{o}_t), \\ \mathbf{o}_{t+1} = \mathbf{o}(K_t, \mathbf{o}_t), \end{cases}$$

with a steady state $(K^*, \mathbf{o}^*)$ such that $K^* = (K^*, \mathbf{o}^*)$ and $\mathbf{o}^* = (K^*, \mathbf{o}^*)$.

Step 1: Linearization
Linearizing around the steady state gives

$$\begin{bmatrix} K_{t+1} - K^* \\ \mathbf{o}_{t+1} - \mathbf{o}^* \end{bmatrix} = J \begin{bmatrix} K_t - K^* \\ \mathbf{o}_t - \mathbf{o}^* \end{bmatrix},$$

where the Jacobian matrix J is:

$$J = \begin{bmatrix} k_K - k_{\mathbf{o}} \\ \mathbf{o}_K - \mathbf{o}_{\mathbf{o}} \end{bmatrix} \begin{bmatrix} \dfrac{\partial k}{\partial K_t} & \dfrac{\partial k}{\partial \mathbf{o}_t} \\ \dfrac{\partial \mathbf{o}}{\partial K_t} & \dfrac{\partial \mathbf{o}}{\partial \mathbf{o}_t} \end{bmatrix}_{(K^*, \mathbf{o}^*)}$$

Step 2: Eigenvalues
The characteristic equation of J is:

$$\lambda^2 - tr(J)\lambda + \det(J) = 0$$

where $tr(J) = k_K + \phi_0$ and $\det(J) = k_K\phi_0 - k_0\phi_K$

Step 3: Stability Conditions
The fixed point (K^*, ϕ^*) is locally stable if both eigenvalues of J lie inside the unit circle, which requires:

$$1 + \det(J) - tr(J) > 0, 1 - \det(J) > 0$$

Conversely, instability occurs if at least one eigenvalue satisfies $|\lambda| > 1$.
A sufficient condition for instability is:

$$\det(J) > 1,$$

because in this case, the product of the eigenvalues exceeds 1 in modulus, ensuring at least one eigenvalue is outside the unit circle.

Economic Interpretation of det(*J*) > 1
The determinant $\det(J) = k_K\phi_0 - k_0\phi_K$ captures the strength of mutual feedback between capital K_t and sentiment ϕ_t:

- $k_0 > 0$: optimism boosts capital formation;
- $\phi_K \neq 0$: changes in capital affect future sentiment (positively in booms or negatively via overinvestment fears);
- k_K, ϕ_0: persistence of capital and sentiment.

When $\det(J) > 1$, the cross-effects are so strong that a small deviation from equilibrium in either sentiment or capital amplifies over time, rather than converging back.

This condition reflects self-reinforcing boom–bust dynamics: rising sentiment fuels capital growth, which in turn reinforces sentiment, until the system overshoots and becomes unstable.

References

Guvenen, F. (2017). Comment on 'Macroeconomics and household heterogeneity'. In M. Eichenbaum & J. A. Parker (Eds.), *NBER Macroeconomics Annual 2016* (Vol. 31, pp. 263–279). University of Chicago Press.

Hall, R. E. (2003). "Wage determination and employment fluctuations," NBER Working Paper No. 9967.

MIX
Papier aus verantwortungsvollen Quellen
Paper from responsible sources
FSC® C105338

If you have any concerns about our products,
you can contact us on
ProductSafety@springernature.com

In case Publisher is established outside the EU,
the EU authorized representative is:
Springer Nature Customer Service Center GmbH
Europaplatz 3, 69115 Heidelberg, Germany

Printed by Libri Plureos GmbH
in Hamburg, Germany